THE EVERLASTING EVANGEL
AND
ITS PROGRAM

By

H. H. PETERS, LL.D.

Author of *Charles Reign Scoville: The Man and His Message*

PUBLISHED BY

BETHANY PRESS
ST. LOUIS

DEDICATED TO

ILLINOIS CHRISTIAN MISSIONARY SOCIETY

IN WHOSE SERVICE THESE ADDRESSES
WERE DELIVERED

1067.

INTRODUCTION

A word with regard to the character of the addresses in this book will be in order. The author has made no attempt to write a series of addresses. While a portion of the title of the book deals with the "Program" of "The Everlasting Evangel," yet it ought to be frankly stated that the program is not presented in a consecutive form.

The addresses were delivered at various gatherings of Christian people and leaders in church work. They were delivered before conventions, county, state, national and international; colleges and seminaries; institutes and conferences. Each address is an effort to meet a particular issue now before the church. If I were preparing a book on evangelism, I could make it more "scientific" but I am satisfied it would not be as "humanistic." We would like therefore to ask our readers who spend a little time in the study of the chapters of this book to remember that they were prepared and delivered in the midst of an active life and that in each case the speaker had in mind the one who is trying his best to meet the problem of Christian service in an efficient way.

H. H. PETERS.

CONTENTS

THE EVERLASTING EVANGEL

In him was life; and the life was the light of men.—John 1:4.

Two classes of people talk of the Everlasting Evangel. There are those who want an evangel that will survive a changing theology. And then there are those who want an evangel whose theology will never change. While we are wrangling over terms and their meaning, we may miss an opportunity for service.

"Evangelism" is a great word. It is the key to many of the problems of our modern church. "Evangel" means "good tidings." The word "gospel" means "God-story." "Evangel" and "gospel" are in reality one and the same thing. "Ism" means "doctrine." "Evangelism," therefore, means the doctrine of the gospel. Personally, I like the word "evangelism" much better than the word "revivalism." The latter strictly speaking means the "re-animation of that which is already living but in a state of decline." The former refers primarily to the proclamation of the gospel to the unsaved. We may need a revival in many churches; and I think we do. It is the feeling of some of us, however, that a revival will come more quickly through evangelizing the unsaved than by a

9

direct attack upon those within the fold but dormant.

It is useless to say to this group that the church must be evangelistic. It is either extension or extinction. The church must go on or go out. We have to move to stand. The order to ancient Israel is applicable to the church, "Go forward." I am assuming in this message that all of us, without regard to personal peculiarities or emphasis in preaching, believe in evangelism. We would not be here if we did not.

In speaking of the Everlasting Evangel I am to present four things: (1) An ageless Person, Christ. (2) A universal organism, the Kingdom. (3) An adequate agent, the church. (4) An efficient program, evangelism.

An Ageless Person—Christ

The Jesus of Judea has become the Christ of eternity. We believe in the historical Jesus but our message must reveal the eternal Christ.

The glory of the gospel belongs to Jesus. As one reads the story he stands in the presence of a character extraordinary in sympathy, intellect and purpose. In fact a new type of man is found in Jesus of Nazareth.

Jesus cannot be described in terms of some specific virtue. He includes all virtues. He brings to perfection in himself every type of goodness. He belongs to all time. He is at home in every age. He is comfortable in every place.

His power attracted soldiers; his gentleness drew children to him; his mercy conquered sinners; his fearlessness awakened enthusiasm. His enemies condemned him for qualities which we now exalt as virtues. Other characters are created by circumstances. Jesus made them.

Humanity is divided into sexes. We have the strength of man and the tenderness of woman. No one can call Jesus sexless. Yet in character he stands midway between the sexes. He is as feminine as woman and as masculine as man. He has kingly qualities and queenly virtues. He is just but merciful. He is courageous but submissive. He is mighty but gentle. He is a king but the suffering servant. Christ is the final type of man and woman. He has put into the strength of manhood the gracious gentleness of womanhood. He has elevated and ennobled the ideal of feminine life by showing that tenderness and loving kindness are not inconsistent with dignity and moral courage. The masculine and the feminine unite in the perfect character of Jesus of Nazareth.

Men are differentiated by the races to which they belong. They are limited and defined by racial temper. The people from whom Jesus came were a "separate people." They were clearly marked off from the balance of humanity. Their religion and patriotism circumscribed them. To this day though they wander landless among the nations they are distinct from all and absorbed in none. Jesus came from the Jews but he was not Jewish. He was a combination of Abraham, Moses, David, Isaiah, Jeremiah, but he was more than all these.

He was brought up in Nazareth, a town without reputation. He stood at the center of three civilizations, Hebrew, Greek and Roman. He was merged in none of these. In him there was neither Jew nor Greek, barbarian nor Scythian, bond nor free. He loved to call himself the Son of Man. He is the mediator of races. He is the one true cosmopolitan; the ultimate type of humanity. He will come to all men everywhere. He is the desire of all nations; the first and truest of all internationalists.

Jesus cannot be explained by his surroundings. The age did not produce him. You cannot date the mind of Jesus. He was not simply in advance of his time. He was detached from the special, free from the trammels of every age and at home in one as well as another. The ancient world did not produce him; the modern world has not created him. His intellect spans the centuries. His heart is the heart of God; his realm is eternity. He was for the first century; he will be for the last century.

Jesus cannot be located among social ranks. He was the son of a peasant, but of the house and lineage of David. He awed kings by the majesty of his bearing but washed his disciples' feet. When he died poor women and rich men joined in ministering at his burial. He speaks to the heart of every class but remains an unclassifiable man.

He is the mediator of rank. Any hope of reconciliation rests with him. The saints on the Mount of Transfiguration want to abide with him but the sick and sinners in the valley know that he is their friend. Jesus is the one universal, catholic and typical man, who stands for all and always. He is the hope of the present order and the inspiration of further progress. He is the ageless person whom we must preach, The Everlasting Evangel.

A Universal Organism—The Kingdom

The Kingdom of Heaven is the social expression of the life of Jesus. I believe it was Emerson who said that every great institution is the lengthened expression of some master spirit. Such is the Kingdom of Heaven. It is the social Christ.

Jesus had much to say about the Kingdom. According to him it is the reign of God in human lives and affairs. He did not create this concept but gave it a larger meaning. The Jews for centuries had believed in the coming of the Messiah. The true Israelite looked forward to a kingdom, in which the son of David would reign supreme. His idea was a divine despotism. His conception was an infinite Caesar.

Two things conspired to produce this conviction. First, the Israelite interpreted things literally. Second, he was the object of bitter persecution wherever he went. The Jew made his mistakes, but the world owes him a great debt of gratitude. He was a man of vision and hope. His dreams may have been crude, but he has been a blessing to the race. Abraham is the father of the faithful of every land. Moses is the world's greatest law-giver. Jesus is the Savior of humanity. His race produced these.

Jesus was a Jew, but he was not Jewish. He was an heir of the hope of Israel. He believed the messianic purposes fulfilled in himself. The difference between Jesus and the Jews was marked. He believed in a spiritual kingdom. They looked for a political empire. Later Paul said that the Kingdom of Heaven is righteousness, peace and joy.

Jesus used the idealism at hand. Hence he read into the Kingdom, a larger meaning than anyone had ever had. It was not a military despotism, nor a political institution. It was ethical, proclaiming right relations in human conduct. It was spiritual, making the character of God as revealed in Christ the basis of life. In this Kingdom, truth is the authority; love is the law; and character the badge of supremacy.

The Kingdom of God is perfect. But this perfection does not rest upon the character of its citizenship. It depends upon the King. Does it rest upon the miracles of Jesus? Does it rest upon the teaching of Jesus? Or does it rest upon the perfect character revealed in his life? Jesus performed miracles, taught truth, and lived a perfect life. The perfection of his Kingdom depends upon all. His miracles reveal power. His truth reveals wisdom. His character reveals love. In his perfection he represents God.

Paul spoke of Jesus as the wisdom, righteousness and holiness of God. Because he thus reveals the Father he is our redemption. He has the wisdom to plan; the goodness to inspire; the power to execute. His wisdom is seen in his method of conquest; in the fitness of his message; in his divine optimism; and his willingness to await the verdict of the ages. His goodness is seen in his life of sacrifice; in his program of service; and in his death as the climax of a life of unselfish goodness. His power is seen in his miracles which are triumphs in nature and human nature; and in the potential power of his message to regenerate the soul and redeem the world.

All we can know of God is that he is wise, good and almighty. Jesus is the revelation of God. He brought to human perfection the qualities thus mentioned. He is the incarnation of the infinite Father. The Kingdom is his social expression.

Two parables are especially attractive from the standpoint of life. These are the parables of the leaven and the mustard seed. Subjectively, the Kingdom has to do with the heart. It is pictured by the leaven in the three measures of meal. Objectively, the Kingdom has to do with the world. This is presented in the mustard seed which became a tree.

Leaven is life. Scientifically we are talking of the yeast plant. Leaven increases by multiplying the number of plants. Thus we have a picture of developing life. The Kingdom of God in the heart is the life of God in the heart.

It will vitalize the whole being, even as the whole lump is leavened. Leaven builds up by the process of decomposition. The yeast plant grows by destroying the particles of flour or meal. Love grows in the heart by the process of destroying the imperfect and incomplete.

The grain of mustard seed is a picture of the social extension of the Kingdom. There are many figures of this besides the grain of mustard seed. It is the little stone cut out of the mountain without hands, that moved on and on until it became a mountain and filled the whole earth. It is the New Jerusalem descending from God out of heaven, coming and coming until it arrives as a new heaven and a new earth. This city John saw symbolizes the society that will finally be when the kingdoms of this world have become the Kingdom of Christ.

Democracy is overthrowing a u t o c r a c y. Kings, czars and kaisers are passing away. The free man is taking the place of the slave. Womanhood is honored. Polygamy has gone forever. Equal suffrage has come. Legal prohibition has arrived. The child is occupying a larger place in the thought and affections of the world. We are approaching the end of war.

Yes, the Kingdom of Heaven is coming. By the enthronement of Christ in the heart it comes to the individual. By his enthronement in the world it will come to society. "Thy kingdom come." The Everlasting Evangel demands a universal organism. This we have in the Kingdom of Heaven.

I believe in Jesus Christ, my Lord and Master; and in the Kingdom of Heaven, the social expression of his timeless life.

I believe in the dual idealism of this Kingdom. Individually it is the enthronement of Christ in the heart driving out sin and selfishness. Socially it is reconstructing society, upon the basis of love, with service as the standard of greatness, and sacrifice as the law of conquest.

The law of the Kingdom is sacrificial service inspired by love.

An Adequate Agent—The Church

The Everlasting Evangel demands an adequate agent. This we find in the church of Christ. Jesus said, "I will build my church." In the church of Christ we have a divine institution, with an ageless creed, and an eternal destiny. Jesus is the founder: "Upon this rock I will build my church." He is the creed. He is eternal: the same yesterday and today and forever. No changes are necessary; he is ageless. The gates of hell shall not prevail against it. Jesus is the author and finisher of the church. He is the beginning and the end; the first and the last. The church, founded upon his character, is a brotherhood of souls and is as enduring as the character of God.

Through the church Christ is made known and the Kingdom extended. It is the agent of the Kingdom; it is an adequate one.

Paul speaks of the church as a building, but one that grows. This is a singlar figure. The church is a building. It has a foundation. It has a corner stone. The whole fabric is fitted and closely joined together; but it is a growing building.

This makes it necessary to note the difference between an organization and an organism. We make an organization; an organism grows. One is mechanical; the other is vital. One enlarges from the outside; the other increases from within. One is static; the other is dynamic. The thing Paul had in mind is that the church of Christ is growing in the world and it is doing so because of its connection with God. When the connection is broken the church is dead.

As already stated, the church is divine. This is a mystical physiological fact. No argument is needed to prove the divinity of Christ. This is taken for granted. But the church is his body; he is the head of the church. The head and body are of the same substance. Since Christ is divine, his church is also. It is as living and vital as he. The church is "his body, the completeness of him, who everywhere fills the universe with himself." There is no limit to the church. It is the completeness of Christ. Jesus everywhere fills the universe with himself. His church, being a community of souls redeemed by him, will finally do the same. The church and Christ are one. Through the church he is made known and his social self expressed.

The church is the habitation of God. "In whom you also are being built up together to become a fixed abode for God through the spirit." Again it "is growing so as to form a holy sanctuary in the Lord." The Tabernacle was a place where God met his people. So was the Temple. The altar has always been the meeting-place. The church of Christ is altar, tabernacle and temple. It is the divine sanctuary. It is the dwelling-place of God.

The messianic hope of Israel reached its highest expression in the fifty-third chapter of Isaiah. He reads in vain who fails to see three manifestations of the Messiah here. Israel was a Messiah to the nations of the earth. Her message was the oneness and absoluteness of God. The testimony was delivered even though Israel did not live up to its full realization.

Christ was promised. Any view one may take of prophecy will lead him to the conclusion that Israel expected an individual Messiah and had a complete prophetic picture of him. It may be that some of the prophecies do not mean what we once thought they did. But there are more than three hundred distinct prophecies, or clear intimations, of the coming Messiah. In the fullness of time he came. The word became flesh. He tabernacled among men.

But the Jesus of Judea has become the Christ of eternity. He makes known his will and manifests his leadership through the church, which is his body. Jesus went away that he might come. Bethlehem and Pentecost are mountain peaks of the same redemptive story. He ascended to the Father after finishing his personal ministry, that he might manifest himself everywhere and endlessly. He does this through the church. The church is, therefore, the Messiah of God to mankind to finish the work of Jesus.

Our Everlasting Evangel must have a church alive and alert, full of the spirit of Christ, dominated by his mind and with a program as untrammeled and ageless as his own eternal self.

An Efficient Program—Evangelism

The gospel has been seeking to express itself through the ages. It had its missionary expression in the apostolic age when men and women went everywhere preaching the word. It had its philosophical expression among the fathers in their conflicts with Greek philosophy and oriental mysticism. It had its artistic expression in the great paintings, human efforts at divine ideals. It had its musical expression in the great oratorios of the church, anticipations of infinite harmony. It had its political expression in the Holy Roman Empire, when church and state combined, under the leadership of Charlemagne, undertook the rule of the world. It had its architectural expression in the great cathedrals of Europe, the gospel of the age expressed in stone. It had its military expression in the crusades, organized to take from the enemies of God the tomb of a dead hero. It had its ecclesiastical expression in the Roman Catholic Church, the old Roman Empire rebuilt upon a religious basis, with the pope taking the place of the emperor and the gradation of the officers in the church corresponding exactly to those of the empire. It had its individualistic expression in the Protestant Reformation. It had its literary expression in Milton's "Paradise Lost" and Dante's "Divine Comedy"; one the epic of protestantism, the other the epic of catholicism. It had had its creedal expression in man's effort to reach ultimate conceptions of faith in theological formularies.

But these are only partial expressions of Christianity. The effort of this age ought to be to express Christianity in all the ways of life. Not a partial, but a full expression. The supreme purpose of Christianity is to make earth like heaven, in obedience and love, purity and praise, righteousness and worship. Paul says the eternal purpose of God is "to sum up all things in Christ, the things in the heavens, and the things upon the earth."

Jesus said, "Blessed are the meek for they shall inherit the earth." Not to the warrior, nor the philosopher, nor the magnate, but to the servant is the promise given.

Evangelism is the general term we apply to the effort of the church to enrich the lives of individuals by the enthronement of Christ and to extend the borders of the Kingdom through the agency of the church. To discuss this theme adequately would require a history of Christendom. We can only sketch a few of the outstanding movements and then concern ourselves with modern evangelism and the relationship of the Disciples of Christ to it.

The New Testament in its present form was collected by the church under the impulse of expansion. It is a generally accepted fact that the books of the New Testament were not written chronologically in the order of their appearance in the canon. The present order, however, is logically evangelistic. It opens with a photograph of Jesus in the fourfold gospels, tells the story of the early conquest of the church, then gives the ethics of Christian living and ends with a picture of a conquering and triumphant church. The very order of the New Testament is, therefore, evangelistic.

Acts of Apostles records the passing of the early church from a congregation struggling to avoid becoming a sect of Judaism until it reaches the outer borders of the Roman Empire as the church of Jesus Christ without caste or limitations. The commission was given in Acts as an order to begin in Jerusalem, go throughout Judea, into and beyond Samaria and to the uttermost parts of the earth. The record of Luke in Acts is a commentary on this program. Peter on Pentecost; Stephen in his defense; Philip in Samaria and in conversation with the Ethiopian statesman; Peter at the household of Cornelius; Paul and Silas in Philippi; Apollos being instructed by Aquila and Priscilla; the defenses and labors of Paul in the closing portions of the Acts—this is the record of the unfolding evangelistic activity of the apostolic church.

The post-apostolic fathers were evangelistic; but not in the same way as the apostles and earlier preachers. Theirs was largely a message of defense, interpretation and literary propaganda. A careful reading, however, of the fathers will reveal a marvelous spirit of evangelistic expansion.

The early church waged three great conflicts —with the Jews, the Greeks, and the Romans. The church was victorious in all. There is always a defeat with every victory and the church lost much of its ceremonial simplicity in its battle with Judaism. It lost the singleness of its intellectual statement in its conflict with Greek philosophy. It lost a large amount of its democracy in its battle with the Roman Empire. By the end of the fifth century the Roman Empire as an institution had almost disappeared but the Roman Catholic Church had appeared. The Roman Catholic Church is the old Roman Empire rebuilt upon a religious basis with the pope taking the place of the Emperor and the gradation of the officers in the church corresponding exactly to those of the

ancient empire. Then came a period called the
Dark Ages—a period about which we know but
little and concerning which we do not have
proper appreciation.

It is not the purpose of this paper to discuss
the evangelism of the Dark Ages but as we
view it there are clearly two lines of activity.

1. Throughout this period Jesus was interpreted as a baron who had his castle on the
hills of eternity, or a king who looked down in
almighty power from the embattlemented walls
of the Holy City. Religion on its objective side
was a form of holy militarism and the triumph
of the church was expected to come about
through imperialistic conquest. The Crusades
are an illustration of this. The crowning of
Charlemagne on Christmas Day, in the year 800,
is especially illustrative of the feeling of the
people at that time. It was the current belief
that the church and state under the leadership
of the Great Charles would unite in the joint
government of the world and that the authority
of the church would be maintained by the
sword. In an old book I used while a student
in college there was a picture of one of the con-
quests of Charlemagne. At the bottom of this
picture is the significant expression, "Charlemagne inflicting baptism upon the people." He

made members by pressure and extended the cause of religion by infliction.

2. On the personal side religion took the form of subjective pietism. The monastery and cloister became popular and saints were recluses. This is not according to the canons of evangelism today but this type of Christian extension developed and preserved art and literature and saved the Bible from the violent hands of vandals. It would be interesting if one could take the time to make a study of the evangelistic activities of the Middle Ages.

The Protestant Reformation, not created but made effective by Martin Luther, inaugurated the modern movement of evangelistic and missionary activity. It began by sounding the note of democracy in religion. The songs of religion it has created are the battle hymns of spiritual conquest. It has inspired missionary activity and has produced great agencies for missionizing and evangelizing the races of mankind. We are coming to see that the continuous Protestant Reformation with its four great characters: Luther, Calvin, Wesley and Campbell, is the voice of God speaking through his church, "Go forward."

It seems to me that the one note that sums up the extension of the cause of Christ today might well be that semi-hackneyed term, "Educational Evangelism." This work must not be limited to organizing training classes for soul-winning, nor elementary courses in the primary elements of religion. It is more than Sunday school work. The viewpoint of modern religious education is that the church of Jesus Christ is and of a right ought to be an educational unit in religion. The whole program from the local church to the larger interests of the Kingdom ought to be instituted and extended along the lines of educational activity.

What should be the position of the Disciples of Christ on the matter of evangelism? Where is our place in the midst of this ceaseless and ageless activity? This depends upon what the objective of the Disciples is. We have said and have repeated it that our purpose is the restoration of primitive, apostolic Christianity. Sometimes we have added the word "essential." Whatever may have been the meaning of this expression at one time, today it has that larger meaning which maintains that we are to restore the spirit of the first century, that we are to proclaim the ageless Christ without trammels or limitations, that under our leadership the gospel of Christ shall accomplish the same thing for the twentieth century that it did for the first. If we can by rallying the forces of Christendom succeed in restoring Christ to his rightful place in human affairs, in order that the twentieth century achievements may duplicate those of the first century, we will restore primitive apostolic and essential Christianity.

Christianity has been an evangelizing agency from Pentecost to this hour. It was a marked characteristic of the first century. Christianity was youthful then but it is still young. Jesus Christ is the same yesterday and today and forever. He is the alpha and omega, the beginning and the end, the first and the last. Our job is to proclaim, not the Jesus of Judea alone, but the Christ of eternity. In the light of this the plea of our people has a new meaning and a strength we have never known before. We are not religious mechanics, nor static theologians; but when we reveal our real selves, we are preachers of an everlasting evangel as young as the first aspiration of man and as abiding as the benediction of God.

I would submit, therefore, that four things must be prominent in our everlasting evangel: (1) An ageless Person, Christ. (2) A universal organism, the Kingdom. (3) An adequate agent, the church. (4) An efficient program, evangelism.

I am thinking of an interview between Caesar and one of his trusted courtiers. "Go," says Caesar, "and find out what the Christians believe." The courtier takes his departure and after some investigation finds a group of Christians, a secluded colony of the saints of the Lord. This is the interview. "Where is your capital?" "We have no capital." "Where is your country?" "We have no country." "What are the boundaries of your province?" "We have no province and no boundaries." "What is your caste?" "We have no caste." "What is your language and color?" "We have no language; no color." "What do you have? Who are you?" "We are followers of the Nazarene; we are Christians." The courtier returns with this story.

With this report began the most relentless and cruel persecution in the annals of Christian history. Rome, tolerant with all religions, annexing the gods along with the provinces, became the bitter foe of Christians and undertook the annihilation of the church. The reason is apparent. It was one internationalism against another. The die was cast. It was the internationalism of love and peace and righteousness against the internationalism of might, money and monarchism. Instinctively Caesar felt that the church had to be crushed or his power would be overthrown.

The church was triumphant because it trusted in God and lived according to the law of love. We have the same task today the church has ever had, the evangelization of the world in our generation. There will be sorrows to endure and conflicts to wage, but the day of the Lord will come. An everlasting evangel gives a message for every age.

THE NEW TESTAMENT: A MANUAL OF EVANGELISM

And there are also many other things which Jesus did, the which if they should be written every one, I suppose that even the world itself would not contain the books that should be written.—John 21:25.

Evangelism has produced many types of literature. There is a large collection of tracts and treatises on what we call personal work or personal evangelism. Some writers have taken the pains to give us books on the whole program for holding a series of evangelistic meetings. I have read many of these with profit and have entered the field myself with a book entitled, *Charles Reign Scoville: The Man and His Message.*

Naturally I am favorable to helps of this kind; but I believe the best book on how to hold a revival meeting is the New Testament itself. What I want to do in this address is to present the New Testament as a manual of evangelism.

The New Testament is arranged in a normal order and is so thoroughly in harmony with the processes of Kingdom growth that many students believe that in its orderly arrangement and perpetuity it is providential. It is not my purpose to discuss this matter. I prefer to leave that to others; but before we have completed the message I hope it will appear that without a doubt the New Testament presents the unfoldment of the program by which the church is to be enlarged and the world saved.

There has never been unanimous agreement among scholars as to the chronological order of the books of the New Testament. One of the best, as well as one of the most recent, gives the order as follows: Thessalonians, Galatians, First Corinthians, Second Corinthians, Romans, Philippians, Philemon, Colossians, Ephesians, the Gospel according to Mark, the Gospel according to Matthew, the Gospel according to Luke, Acts of the Apostles, Revelation, Hebrews, First Peter, James, the Letters of John, the Gospel according to John, the Letters to Timothy and to Titus, Jude, and Second Peter.

In presenting the evangelistic message of the New Testament, four things are essential: A picture of Jesus; the development of the church; the application of the message to the needs of the world; the prophecy of a growing and triumphant church. In other words we must answer four questions: (1) Who is Jesus? (2) How may we enter his church? (3) What must we do as Christians, having taken membership in the church? (4) What is the outcome of the church?

The Photograph

The method of writing the life of Christ has changed considerably from Edersheim to Papini. In the old days the method was biographical. Today it is artistic. Our forefathers were interested in the biography of Jesus. We are interested in seeing Jesus. We want a picture. "Behold the Man." This is the motive that moves us in the study of Christ.

The only danger in a message of this kind is that we may make it too extensive. But I do want to get before us the photograph of Jesus as it is given in the fourfold gospel. There are two things about Christ that we must come to see: what he did and who he was. The study of what he did comes under two heads: his utterances and his conduct. Matthew gives the utterances; Mark his conduct. Luke and John both deal with his personality. To Luke Jesus was the perfect man; to John he was the eternal Christ. In the fourfold gospel, therefore, we have not only the Messiah who fulfilled the prophecies and revealed his power, but a perfect character who is the ageless Son of the eternal Father.

Jesus is the Man in the Book. The testimony of Jesus is the spirit of the Bible. He is the alpha and the omega, the beginning and the end, the first and the last. While Jesus is introduced to us in the entire Bible, it is the four-fold gospel of Matthew, Mark, Luke and John that gives his photograph. "A river went out from Eden to water the garden, and from thence it was parted, and became four heads."—Genesis 2:10. The gospel is one river, parting and becoming four streams. Follow these streams and you will come to the united single river of life—the gospel of Christ.

MATTHEW'S MESSAGE

Matthew might have taken for his text Zechariah 9:9, "Behold, thy king." He introduces Jesus as the son of David and of the seed of Abraham. His narrative is called "the book of the generation of Jesus Christ." The ancestry of Jesus is an important consideration. Matthew was a Jew and an official of the Roman Empire. He was collecting taxes when Jesus called him. He soon made a feast for his new Master. He saw in him the fulfillment of prophetic promises and Jewish hopes. The messiahship is his theme. Everything contributes to this end. The seed of Abraham is to sit on the throne of David. He quotes at least one hundred Old Testament predictions to show that Jesus is the Messiah. To him all these prophecies and types are fulfilled in Jesus of Nazareth.

Matthew's gospel was early called "The Oracles." The reason for this is that fully one-half of it is made up of the addresses and utterances of Jesus, the sayings of the King. The Sermon on the Mount is given in its fullest form in Matthew 5, 6 and 7. The parables of the Kingdom loom large in this book.

Matthew wrote the national gospel, or the gospel of the Kingdom. He uses the expression, "Kingdom of heaven," something like thirty times. He records fourteen of our Lord's parables and eleven of them begin with the expression, "The kingdom of heaven is like." In this gospel John the Baptist comes preaching, "Repent for the kingdom of heaven is at hand." Jesus continues the same emphasis. Thus Matthew, dealing with the past, wrote to prove that Jesus is the Messiah and rejected King. He shows the purpose of the Law and how Jesus came to fulfill it. In any presentation of Jesus this must be first. He must be first of all the Messiah, of the seed of Abraham and the son of David.

Mark's Message

Mark might have taken as his text these words of Isaiah 42:1, "Behold, my servant." Mark himself was a servant of the Lord and a minister. Paul writes, "Take Mark and bring him with thee for he is profitable to me for the ministry.'' The order of his gospel is the one common to the first three gospels. It was probably the first one written and this accounts for its dominant order. While Matthew diverges from Mark's order, Luke converges to it. Both follow it fundamentally. Mark probably wrote for the Roman element of society, or at least the Gentile Christians, who were looking for a deliverer. He paid but little attention to prophecies and their fulfillment. These were men looking for a great worker, organizer and conqueror. Mark shows the deeds of Jesus surpassed those of Caesar.

The events in the life of our Lord are passed in rapid succession. He records no long sermons; gives no genealogy; makes no reference to the miraculous birth; passes the adoration of the wise men; mentions no boyhood at Nazareth; does not include the visit to Jerusalem at the age of twelve; neither does he refer to the pre-existence of Jesus with the Father.

Mark introduces his book as the ''beginning of the gospel of Jesus Christ, the Son of God.'' His purpose is to prove the divinity of Jesus by the works of his ministry. He is the ''Mighty God,'' the One before whom all must bow. He is Caesar raised to the *nth* power, but infinite

in compassion as well as power. Matthew's
Messiah is the Mighty King of Mark.

Luke's Message

Luke might have taken for the text of his
message Zechariah 6:12, "Behold, the man."
His theme is Jesus, the Man. Luke was an educated Greek physician. Paul calls him, "The
beloved physician." He labored with Paul in
his missionary tours among the Gentiles. Being
a Greek he was seeking the Perfect Man. He
found him in Jesus of Nazareth. Luke makes
but little reference to the fulfillment of Old
Testament prophecies. The Gentiles in general
would not be interested in them. The Greeks
regarded one of superior intellect, becoming
habits, and graceful action as nearest their
ideal.

Luke gives prominence to the human feelings
of Christ. He uses the name "Jesus" two hundred forty-six times. He gives in detail the
circumstances of the birth and infancy of the
Holy Child. He alone records the three songs
of the nativity. Luke tells how the child grew;
how he increased in wisdom and stature, and
in favor with God and man; how he was subject unto his parents. He explains that the
doctors were astonished at his understanding
and answers. Thus Luke shows how Jesus lived

as a man, that he might in his own life bring us near to God. He records the sermon in the synagogue in Nazareth in which Jesus announces his life's mission. He alone records the story of the penitent thief and the prodigal son. Of the twenty-two miracles he records, seventeen of them are cures. Luke gives four miracles unnoted by the other writers, and they are all special cures effected by the Divine Physician. They are the widow's son raised; the crooked woman made straight; the curing of the dropsy; and restoring the ear which Peter severed in the garden.

He gives fourteen parables not found in other gospels. They deal with the problems of human life and duty. Among these are the Good Samaritan, the Prodigal Son and the Rich Man and Lazarus. This is the gospel of prayer. At his baptism Jesus was praying when the Holy Spirit came upon him. The choice of the Twelve followed a night of prayer. Fifteen times in this gospel we are brought to see the prayer life of Jesus. It is Luke who tells us that his first and last words upon the cross were prayers.

JOHN'S MESSAGE

A good text for John's message, if he had chosen one, would have been Isaiah 40:9, "Behold, your God." John's theme is Immanuel,

God with us. He identifies Jesus with God. John was the youngest of the Twelve and is spoken of as the "one whom Jesus loved." His gospel must have been written much later than the other three. John has a special message for the church. His is a book on Christian evidences. He records numerous conversations with Jesus and shows the Master often among his friends. From beginning to end he represents Jesus as the incarnate God. He says that his gospel was written to prove that Jesus is the Christ.

He makes use of the word "believe" one hundred one times; of the word "life" sixty-five times; and the word "signs" forty-seven times. Jesus calls God his Father twenty-one times in Matthew, three times in Mark, and eleven times in Luke; only thirty-five times in the first three gospels. But in John Jesus calls God his Father one hundred eight times.

Jesus talks of the Father's house, emphasizing the domestic and filial rather than the regal and kingly. John gives nineteen personal interviews with Jesus. Among them is the important one with Nicodemus.

APPLICATION

Matthew gives the gospel of the past; Mark of the present; Luke of the future; and John of eternity. Thus the fourfold gospel includes all time and presents the eternal Christ. Matthew introduces Jesus as the Messiah of the Jews; Mark as the Mighty King; Luke as the Perfect Man; and John as the Eternal Savior.

While these writers present the story from different angles they agree on the great issues of the career of Jesus. The Promised King; the Divine Servant; the Perfect Man; and the Son of God who suffers and dies, this is the divine order. But the Promised King, Divine Servant, Perfect Man and Son of God rises and thus it is revealed in completeness.

Jesus speaks the word of God; does his work; reveals his ideal of manhood; and now lives with him in the eternal order. His photograph is the God-man.

The Institution

The Book of Acts was written by Luke to Theophilus and purports to tell "all that Jesus began both to do and teach." It is a continuation of Luke's gospel story for he addressed this communication to the same individual.

We are probably as familiar with Acts as any book in the New Testament. Every revival meeting ought to think through the first chapter and note especially the commandment of Jesus that his disciples should not depart from

Jerusalem but should wait for the promise of the Father. In our anxiety to tell inquiring sinners what they must do to be saved, we sometimes miss the point of the second chapter. This chapter is the record of the birthday of the church. "They were all with one accord in one place." Peter preached; a multitude heard the gospel. The triumphant declaration of the preacher, that God had made Jesus both Lord and Christ, brought conviction. A definite answer was given those who sought salvation. The church on this first day had a message for the outsiders: "Repent, and be baptized every one of you in the name of Jesus Christ for the remission of sins, and he shall receive the gift of the Holy Spirit." It had a program for the insiders: "And they continued steadfastly in the apostles' doctrine and fellowship, in the breaking of bread, and in prayers."

Then this wonderful little book continues to tell the story of the work of the church. It is the first effort at church history and is naturally the most important.

The commission as it is recorded in Acts 1:8 reads as follows, "But ye shall receive power, after that the Holy Spirit is come upon you: and ye shall be witnesses unto me both in Jerusalem, and in all Judea, and in Samaria, and unto the uttermost part of the earth." The

Book of Acts is commentary on this commission. Chapters 1 to 7 deal with the conquest of the gospel in Jerusalem; chapters 8 to 12 in Judea and Samaria; chapters 13 to 28 tell of the success of the gospel among the nations. Thus we have in the Book of Acts the account of the establishment and development of the church of Christ in the world. It records how men and women came to Christ in the early days of the church.

It is the book of conversions and gives ten or twelve specific examples and refers to many others. These stories of the triumph of the gospel in human life are worth more to us today than all the fantastic experiences ever worked out by human ingenuity. I have the feeling that if these stories were published as individual accounts of the workings of the gospel they would be very helpful as tracts on how to reach people today.

We have had some trouble in understanding the work and operation of the Holy Spirit, but a careful study of the Book of Acts will clear up many things connected with this matter. I would recommend its reading not only to find an answer to the question, ''What must I do to be saved?'' but also an answer to another question equally fundamental, ''How does God work by his Spirit today?''

THE LIFE

Of the twenty-seven books of the New Testament, twenty-one were written definitely about the Christian life. These letters deal with every phase of Christian experience and cover all the problems that the early church confronted. It is fortunate indeed for us that the writers of these messages did not proclaim laws. They presented principle. Because of this the New Testament lives and will abide.

We make a mistake that almost becomes a blunder when we make the New Testament a book of law rather than a collection of principles. Naturally a code is more easily handled than such a volume as the New Testament; but it soon becomes useless for the race outgrows it.

The evangelist must use precaution in handling these great documents written by men of God under the impulse of the Spirit. Sometimes a sentence will meet the issue. Again a chapter will do this. Frequently an entire book may be used to present and illustrate a single idea. There is no doubt in the mind of one who has studied with any degree of care the books of the New Testament but what each one has a fundamental and specific purpose. About the best preaching one can do is to take a book and give its meaning in a single address. It can then be broken up into its component parts with ease and accuracy.

Let me illustrate what I mean. The Epistle to the Ephesians has a central theme, a keynote. Paul says here that the middle wall of partition between the Jew and Gentile was broken down, that God might make of the two one new humanity, and thus bring peace. In an age when race prejudice and jealousy are so prominent Ephesians becomes good material for a sermon. The Epistle to the Galatians deals with liberty and while there are many interesting items in it, the one outstanding message is liberty in Jesus Christ. In Hebrews we have the romance of ceremonialism. This seems to have been originally a sermon or an address but found its way into the New Testament because of its value. Here Jesus is contrasted with the great personalities of time and eternity and is equal with God. He is the same yesterday and today and forever. Time will not permit us in an address of this kind to go further into detail about book studies, but I especially commend this type of work as most fruitful and useful.

I am not saying that we should not have tracts and booklets on the various phases of Christian life and service; but my contention is that the New Testament is the best volume

ever printed on how to live this life. We need
a revival of study of this book, not alone for
the purpose of proving that the things are true,
but for the further intention of showing how
the Christian may walk and talk with his Lord.

The Goal

Nearly every preacher has had an ambition
to understand and explain the Book of Revelation. In the early days of my ministry I read
several of the best known books on Revelation.
They did me good but kept me changing my
mind so often that I really did not have time
to become a crank about any particular viewpoint. I have come to feel that the Book of
Revelation does not apply to any particular age
but portrays the perennial conflict between good
and evil. It was for the age in which the
Roman Empire was the oppressor; the age in
which the Roman church was the oppressor;
the age in which absolutism in government was
the oppressor; and it will be used in every age
in which evil undertakes to control the destinies
of the race. From this standpoint the Book of
Revelation has much of splendid preaching
value. At a time when democracy is trying to
assert itself and when thrones of every kind are
crumbling this is a book of special importance.

The Book of Revelation is the climax of Utopianism. It is a great dream book and belongs, from the standpoint of literature, to those great books like Plato's "Republic," Moore's "Utopia," and others. But there is no comparison as to their relative value. The Book of Revelation is complete. It has the final word. John saw a multitude going to heaven but he saw something besides this. While on the lonely isle of Patmos there was a rift in the clouds and he saw the New Jerusalem descending from God out of heaven. It kept coming and coming until finally it came and there was a new heaven and a new earth and God himself dwelt with men.

Our preaching must have the note of hope. We must believe in our message and its final triumph. We cannot secure recruits for a lost cause. The cargo of a sinking ship loses its value very rapidly. If this world is a sinking ship it will be very difficult to arouse much enthusiasm over it. But it is not. It is God's world. He has invested much in it. He will bring it out right at last. There will be a new heaven and a new earth. The New Jerusalem will come. The purpose of the preacher is to arouse an interest in a winning and victorious enterprise.

Conclusion

The New Testament is a sermon within itself. Just as many a word in it or a clause or a sentence or a paragraph or a book has a sermon, so the New Testament as a collection of the letters of the new covenant is itself a sermon. It has four divisions. First of all, is the photograph of Jesus given in Matthew, Mark, Luke and John. Then there is the presentation of the church which is the social expression of his timeless and ageless life. This is given in the Acts. Following this we have the letters telling us how to walk with Jesus and exemplify our conduct in the world as well as the sanctuary. The sermon comes to a close, just as a symphony reaches its climax, with the note of hope, announcing that the kingdoms of this world have become the Kingdom of Christ and that God is all and in all in human life and society.

PRIESTS, LOGICIANS OR PROPHETS?

He that prophesieth edifieth the church.—1 Corinthians 14:4.

Religion has been defined as the life of God in the soul of man. This is not comprehensive but it is a good starting point. It means that religion is essential and abiding. As Sabatier says, "Man is incurably religious." Religion begins in the soul of man. Revelation is God coming down; religion is man coming up. God and man meet in religion. The Father and the child are then one.

Temples and altars, creeds and rituals, songs and sermons are but manifestations of religion. Religion is aided by these, but is not dependent upon them. Religion existed before creeds were written or temples erected. The altar did not create religion. Religion came from the soul by way of the altar.

In the study of religion we find three prominent elements. These have produced distinct types: the priest, the logician and the prophet. A man's religion usually takes one form or the other. Sometimes it is a singular combination of these various forms.

THE PRIEST

A priest presupposes a temple, an altar and a sacrifice. It is impossible to have a priest without these. This is seen in the Old Testa-

ment. In the Tabernacle and Temple services
the priestly idea was prominent. In fact the
priestly was predominant in all ancient religion.
It is found today in catholicism as an institution and in many forms of protestantism. Many
members of protestant churches are essentially
Roman Catholic and many Roman Catholics
have the spirit of protestantism. When your
religion is dependent upon a priest or preacher,
you are a ritualist; in Christian terminology, a
Romanist.

With the priestly the ceremony is everything.
Character is incidental. The priest is an attor-
ney to be employed. God is a Judge and heaven
is a supreme court. The priest either forgives
sins or has it done. To the Catholic he forgives
them. To the priestly protestant he has it done.
These are identical in spirit and aim. Pharisaism in the time of Jesus was priestly. It insti-
tutionalized religion and made form the end.
It is the same with Pharisaism today.

THE LOGICIAN

The logician has a creed. He maintains by
mathematical exactness that his religion is true.
He spends his time proving that his religion is
the correct and only one. He reads everybody
out of the church who does not agree with him.

Creeds were written by scholars to define the faith. The man who does not accept the definition is condemned. The scribes at the time of Jesus belonged to this school. Protestantism today is largely of this character. It first defines, then defends. Its hope is in literary accuracy. Correct intellect is the goal; conformity in thinking the aim.

With the logician the creed is all that counts. A heretic is dangerous. Freedom of thought is denied. Even character has but little consideration. It is what you believe, not what you are, that saves you. While the priest might burn a man for refusing to comply with his ritual, the logician brands him for refusing to believe his creed. Burning is more painful, but branding is as dangerous.

The Prophet

The prophet is the highest type of religious leader. A prophet does not necessarily draw maps of the future. He may do this, but it is not an essential part of his work. Prophecy is teaching. All true teaching is prophecy. If any man hath a prophecy let him prophesy.

The prophet is usually irregular from the standpoint of the conservative who says, "Hands off," "Let well enough alone." He doesn't want to be disturbed. He would not

object to a reform if it were here, but he dreads
the birth-pains essential to bringing it. The
prophets of Israel were heretics. They were
more than reformers; they were revolutionists.
They started out, not to change the law of the
land, but to apply it in a new way. They were
determined to direct the current of history.
They denounced the priestly in unmeasured
terms and went far beyond the intellectualism
of the rabbis. They were preachers of truth;
they were teachers of righteousness. The true
religion of Israel is not found in its legalism,
nor in the ceremonialism of the Pharisees, nor
in the intellectual juggling of the scribes; but
in the message of the prophets. They prepared
the way for Jesus.

The error of Jesus from the viewpoint of the
establishment was that he carried to perfection
the righteousness of the prophets. He spoke
as one having authority. The people detected
at once the difference between his method and
that of the scribes. He found his authority in
his consciousness of God, not in outside ceremonies, nor doctrinal statements. The scribes
despised him and the Pharisees hated him. The
priests believed him to be the enemy of God
and man. But when religious millinery has
been thrown away and doctrinal machinery
abandoned, the free prophetic spirit of Jesus

will be in the world as its leaven and life. Jesus still lives and his truth abides because he was neither a priest nor a logician, but a living prophet.

With the prophet character is the essential thing. Humanity is divine. Personality is power. God is living. The prophet does not condemn correct thinking, but makes the formation of character the end of doctrine. He maintains that doctrine is Christian when it produces Christian character.

THE CHURCH

To appreciate these principles it will be necessary to apply them in several ways. The church has great value. It has a growing place in the heart of the world. It will help in our understanding of the church and its mission to view it from the three angles mentioned.

The priestly idea of religion regards the church as an organization made up of two classes: priests and laymen. The priests are the attorneys and the laymen are the clients. Salvation depends upon relationship to the organization. The church of the priest is not patterned after the simple democracy of the New Testament, but after the Roman Empire or the Aaronic priesthood. Monarchy in religion is essential to priestliness. This is one of the most seductive and dangerous of all the fallacies of this world. It is so simple to become a member of an organization. It is so easy to lose individuality in a big machine. Many an intelligent man is perfectly willing to throw himself upon the bosom of an organization that agrees to do his thinking and stand sponsor for him when he crosses over. This idea of the church is not limited to any particular religious body. It seems to be peculiar to a certain type of mind; a type that is immature and primitive.

The logician regards the church as a debating society, in which truth is reached by discussion and argumentation. The creed is forged in the flames of animated speech and when it is given to the church it must be defended at all hazards. Alas, how deceiving is this! The history of the church is replete with argument and discussion. Men have tried to reach ultimate conceptions of truth in debating societies when passions were inflamed and minds dwarfed. The man who refuses to believe a creed thus prepared, is thrown out of respectable society here and has the door closed in his face over there.

The prophet regards the church as a growing institution. It questions anything that claims to be fixed. Even the idea of God is progres-

sive. God is made known to us as eternal, then
paternal, now fraternal. The prophet thinks
of the church as the living body of the eternal
Christ. A man's relationship to it depends
upon his vital connection with Jesus as the life
of the world. He accepts as truth the statement of Jesus, "I am the vine and ye are the
branches." Thus a man's membership in the
church of Christ depends, not upon the fee he
gives the priest, nor his endorsement of a set
of tenets, but upon his relationship to Jesus
Christ. The church thus conceived is the body
of Christ and as divine as he.

SALVATION

In the matter of salvation these three ideas
are in open conflict. With the priestly, salvation is purchased by sacrifices; with the logical,
salvation is granted as the reward of orthodoxy;
with the prophetic, salvation is character
formed in comradeship with Jesus Christ.
Priestly salvation was the original. There are
two lines of sacrifice running throughout the
Old Testament, animal sacrifice and human
service. In the beginning animal sacrifice was
in the ascendancy and human service small.
But as we pass through the Old Testament the
one declines while the other increases. When
we come to the New Testament, we find Jesus

of Nazareth, the Lamb of God and the Suffering
Servant. As the story of his career unfolds, we
lose sight of the sacrificial and stand in the
presence of the Great Servant who saves by
serving.

The logical very early manifested itself. The
New Testament has a large element of the
polemical. Paul and others had to engage in
arguments with Jews, Greeks and Romans. But
the prophetic, which made salvation depend
upon character, came into prominence before
the end of the apostolic age. And as the spirit
of Jesus Christ takes possession of the world,
we shall find that the prophetic will grow yet
more and more to the displacement of all in-
ferior forms.

THE BIBLE

There is also a difference in view concerning
the Bible. To the priest, the Bible is a book of
ceremonies. To the logician, it is a system of
doctrines. To the prophet, it is a book of life.
There is a great gulf fixed between the priest
and the prophet with respect to the Bible. To
think of the Bible as a book of marvelous and
overawing ceremonies has been helpful to some,
and many of the artistic conceptions of life are
born of the spirit. The mind revels in the
ceremonies of the tabernacle and the temple.

There is something of surpassing beauty to the reverent soul in the ritual of a high church. But neither art nor fear are final motives in religion.

The logician, too, is pleased with himself and with the Bible he creates. Some in criticizing this idea of religion have gone so far as to say that every logician makes his own Bible. It sometimes looks like it. We have been warned that man by searching cannot find out God. But we keep trying. We work out logical syllogisms and processes of reasoning. We try to prove the existence of God and the nature of his character. We tell how the world was made and prove it. Wise men try to explain the relationship of the persons of the Trinity and the dual nature of Jesus. They give us positive assurances on the philosophy of the atonement and claim a perfect understanding of the ways of God to man. The creeds of the church were born of this spirit. They were written to explain things; to define things; to prove things. But a creed is scarcely finished until the minority repudiates it and then it all has to be done over. A new creed is made.

To the prophet, the Bible is a book of life and the living word. The characters of the Old Testament are not dead saints but living preachers. The Bible is not the stenographic notes of the private secretaries of the Almighty; but a living message that came up out of the lives of great and good men and out of the heart of the chosen nation, inspired and directed of God. The Bible claims for itself, that holy men spoke as they were moved by the Holy Spirit. It nowhere states that they wrote as they were dictated to by the Holy Spirit. The prophet of God makes the word living and powerful, sharper than a two-edged sword. He believes that the words of Jesus are spirit, that they are life.

The Church Building

Naturally the church building will be formed according to the convictions of the time. When men emphasize the ceremonial, they will build cathedrals. The cathedral is the highest architectural expression of the priestly idea. The protest against this, passing from the formal to the intellectual, resulted in the meeting-house. Today we are becoming dissatisfied with the meeting-house. We find that it is not sufficient. The cathedral was built for the display of the ritual; the meeting-house for the defense of the creed. These do not satisfy the modern man. We want the beauty of the cathedral and the pulpit of the meeting-house; but we demand an educational institution. The prophetic spirit demands that we shall build for the training of souls, both old and young, in the essentials of religion. A priest might be contented and find joy in the humble service of a great cathedral; a logician might be satisfied to spend his days thundering forth arguments to the intellects of men, proving the great doctrines of religion; but a prophet of God, who believes in the power of truth taught and who knows that true religion can grow just as fast, and no faster, as men advance in the knowledge of the Lord, will construct a different type of building for his work.

EVANGELISM

These principles apply to evangelism. Priestly religion does not hold revivals. It relies primarily upon changing the relationship of the individual in babyhood. When a "mission" is held for adults, the chief aim is to call the community to submission to the ritual. The logician goes to the other extreme. Modern revivalism had its origin in an argument and for a long time this was its chief asset. In these days declaration has taken the place of argument but the principle is much the same. With the prophetic evangelism deals with character. The program is twofold: (1) to save from sin and (2) to save from sinning. The method is by teaching. The work of the church is carried on in such a way, that the young will come to the knowledge of the Lord through teaching and adults will grow in grace as they grow in knowledge.

Thus we have two methods of evangelism: (1) the cultural and (2) conversional. Both may be made to harmonize with the prophetic spirit of religion. Under the cultural method children grow up in the nurture and admonition of the Lord, and are never conscious of those great radical changes which come to the sinning. In reality the conversional must also follow the same method, for as Jesus says, except the sinner turn and become as a little child he cannot enter into the Kingdom of God. When the principle of teaching is fully recognized the growth of Christianity will be marvelous.

THE TWO LAWS OF LEARNING

There are two laws of learning: First, he who knows will do; second, he who does will know. The first emphasizes instruction. The second makes experience the chief item. Each law has its champions. Around each is built a philosophy of education. Many of the mistakes in our educational system arise from the fact that we emphasize one of these at the expense of the other. It is not always true that he who knows will do; nor are we certain that he who does will know. Who would think of teaching mathematics by a course of lectures on the multiplication table? We are told, however, that in the matter of chemistry we learn by doing; that we evolve the law by experiments. But even there it takes more than action. Both methods are necessary. The two laws must blend in one.

Education is a unit. Strictly speaking there is no such thing as secular and religious education. What we commonly call religious education is subject to the same principles of procedure as secular education. But the temptation is great here. It is easy to lecture on religion. It is not difficult to tell people what they ought to do. To the surprise of the theorist they will not always do it. The mere impartation of knowledge is not sufficient. If it were we would be much further along than we are, for the church has had plenty of preaching and teaching.

There are two reasons why the church is belated: First, as a rule there is not much purpose in our preaching; second, we do not give sufficient opportunities for the practice of the things we preach. The church needs a program of instruction but a plan of action as well. My appeal is not that we shall have less preaching, but more purpose in it; and then plenty of opportunities for the practical expression of religious instruction. Many of our most capable leaders in religious work have a definite educational program along both lines and are getting specific results. It has been well said that the whole program of education is to put education into religion and religion into education.

In these days we are placing much emphasis on experience in education, and in religious education this is especially true. But experience alone is not sufficient. Just as the pendulum swings from one extreme to the other so the human mind passes from one extreme to the other. We go easily from instruction to social service. The critics of the church tell us that what the church needs to do is to get busy, to help the needy; and that the reflex action of such religious conduct will produce Christian character. There is no greater delusion than this. The work of the Kingdom cannot be accomplished by handing out sandwiches and contributing second-hand garments. Such work may have an important place in an immature community; but this age demands justice, not charity. Nothing is more certain than that it is impossible to generate spiritual life by automatic morality.

Some of the master minds in the realm of education have given us definitions that are worth while. Here are five of the best that I have seen. Spencer, "To prepare us for complete living." Butler, "A gradual adjustment to the spiritual possession of the race." Coe, "An effort to assist immature persons to realize themselves and their destiny as persons." Drawbridge, "Taking one living idea at a time from one's own mind and planting it so that it will grow in the mind of another." DuBois, "Teaching is enabling another to restate the truth in terms of his own life."

In looking over this list carefully one is impressed first with the confusion of ideas, but upon closer examination all confusion vanishes. The whole story may be summed up in the thought, that education is the equipment of the individual to appreciate the world in which he finds himself and to express his life for the betterment of his kind. This to me is religious education. This is the task of the church.

We have been told repeatedly that the two fundamental elements of modern education are the development of the child and the character of the teacher. Human life unfolds naturally and normally. If there is no possibility of normal development then human life is a failure. The Creator intended his creature to gradually become conscious of Himself and the world. Again we are told that teaching must come from experience; that before one can instruct another he must himself have had an experience out of which he speaks. Many books have been written on these fundamental elements of education and in universities elaborate courses of study are outlined to present them. But they are not modern. They were contributed by Christianity. In the normal development of the child Jesus we have the model for growing, developing and enlarging life. Jesus increased in wisdom, in stature and in favor with God and man. He grew physically, intellectually, socially and spiritually. His normal development is the basis of our concept of growing human life.

Then Jesus was the greatest of all teachers. He taught from experience. The men of his day did not understand this. They said he spoke as one "having authority." He spoke from within, out of experience. The scribes pointed out truth, but Jesus revealed it by the way he lived and spoke out of the abundance of his heart. The character of Christ then as a teacher is our inspiration. Truth must be known before it can be revealed.

Some time ago I ran across a very interesting testimonial from Chas. Darwin. Here it is, "Up to the age of thirty, poetry of many kinds gave me great pleasure, and even as a schoolboy I took intense delight in Shakespeare. Formerly pictures gave me considerable and music very great delight. But now for many years I cannot endure to read Shakespeare, and found it so intolerably dull that it nauseated me. I have also almost lost my taste for pictures or music. If I had my life to live again I would make a rule to read some poetry and listen to some music at least once every week; for perhaps the parts of my brain now atrophied would thus have been kept active through use. The loss of these tastes is a loss of happiness, and may possibly be injurious to the intellect and more probably to the moral character, by enfeebling the emotional part of our nature.''

It is clear that while Darwin was a wise man in many respects his education in matters spiritual was neglected. In all probability many theories that we meet frequently would have been different, if Darwin had given as much time to the training of his emotional nature as he did his mental. This is the task of the church, to instruct human life so that its expression in the world will become complete and normal.

In fact there are three laws of learning: (1) He who knows will do. (2) He who does will know. (3) He should know that he may do. The conclusion of the whole matter is this, he who knows the truth that he may live it is educated.

The final force in religion is teaching. Jesus said, "Teaching them to observe all things whatsoever I have commanded you." This is the task of the church, to teach the religion of Jesus Christ. The knowledge of the truth makes freedom known, the expression of the truth makes it a possession.

The priestly may be impressive; the logical may be convincing; but the prophetic will be experienced.

THE TWO FUNDAMENTALS OF EDUCATION

And it came to pass, when Jesus ended these words, the multitudes were astonished at his teachings; for he taught them as one having authority, and not as their scribes.—Matthew 7:28, 29.

And Jesus advanced in wisdom and stature, and in favor with God and men.—Luke 2:52.

For some time we have been classifying education as secular and religious; as non-Christian and Christian. We have not quite been willing to go far enough to say that education is non-Christian; but in our unguarded moments we have said, that certain types of education are Christian. It seems to me that the time has come to have done with this sort of classification.

The two fundamentals of education are the teacher and the pupil. We are familiar with the statement of James A. Garfield to the effect, that Mark Hopkins on one end of a log and a pupil on the other constituted a university. It matters not so much about the size of the school as it does the size of the teacher in the school, and the determination of the pupil. One great teacher and a determined pupil will accomplish results in the realm of education. There is no objection to the size of the school unless we sacrifice thoroughness for numbers.

We frequently hear some distinguished educator say that modern education has invented two theories: First, that the teacher in order to do effective work must teach out of experience; that he must really teach himself; second, that the pupil naturally and normally unfolds to the call of culture; that education is the development of the inner self. We have, therefore, two propositions which fairly represent the modern educational movement.

1. *Modern education maintains that the successful teacher teaches out of experience.*

Before we inquire into the originality of this doctrine, let us discover its meaning. In its meaning we will find one of the most vital lessons of our modern life. The historian must feel the throb of history, and must live again in his own life the life of the race before he can actually teach history. He must have the experience of China before he can teach Chinese history. He must have the experience of Japan before he can teach Japanese history. He must have the experiences of Europe before he can teach European history. To teach history is not to recite a long list of dates; give an outline of the various wars of history, and the battles of the same; or even to tabulate the achievements of great personalities. The historian must live again the life of the world before he can make history vital and real. The mathematician must have an experience of orderliness in his soul to teach mathematics. The geologist must have the consciousness of millenniums to teach geology. The teacher of literature must have an appreciation of the songs and sermons, poems and prose, philosophy and oratory of the people whose literature he would teach.

Christianity stands for exactly the same principle and taught it a long time before the days of modern education. Going back to the first text of this message, we have the statement, "He taught them as one having authority, and not as their scribes." Jesus taught out of experience. He had authority within himself. He could teach peace for he had it. He could teach holiness for he possessed it. He could teach God for he knew him. He could teach of men for he had shared all the essential experiences of the race. He taught as one having authority, and not as the scribes.

The authority of the scribe was external. It always is. He had the text before him, and could point it out. The scribe compelled his disciples to commit to memory certain precepts

and repeat them by rote. He was true to the
statutes, and loyal to the manuscripts. His law
was originally engraved on tables of stone, and
it still belongs to that age. Stones and parch-
ments were final with him. His business was
merely to point out what was said. But the
Great Teacher taught differently. He had the
message within himself. Out of his heart he
spoke. He had authority.

The only thing that modern educators claim
is that they have been capable of the discovery
of the motive and method of Christ. Christianity is the only form of religion or philosophy
that has carried this idea to its final conclusion.
Christ is Christianity and Christianity is Christ.
The message of Christianity is but the expression of the matchless life of its Founder. We
have no hesitancy in commending the leaders of
the modern educational movement for their loyalty to this Teacher. We do, however, object
when we find them stating so emphatically that
this principle of teaching out of experience is
a modern invention. It would be glory enough
for the modern educational movement, if its
advocates were content, to say that they had
merely found the path, and are walking in the
way of the Man of Galilee.

2. *Modern education teaches that human life
develops under instruction, and that one comes*

to culture and character naturally and normally through the educational processes of our day.

Educators maintain that human life is worth while; that it is inherently good; and that education seeks to develop what is naturally and natively within the individual. It has no use for the doctrine of total depravity in either the things of the intellect or the heart. This is a wonderful conception of human life. We ought to be grateful that our universities and colleges are calling our attention to the great fact of man's inherent divinity. There are possibilities in the humblest child. All were created in the likeness and image of God.

But a long time before modern education existed or announced its discovery of the child, we read of one who "advanced in wisdom and stature, and in favor with God and man." This is the record of the unfoldment of the only normal child this world has ever known. It is the story of the child Jesus. So much has been said about his development, that it will pay us to go somewhat into detail in order that we may discover just what he was, and how he came to be such. Luke's statement about him leads us to conclude that his development was physical, intellectual, social and spiritual.

He was a normal physical being. Much of the theology of the world presents Jesus either a

military conqueror or a pious anaemic. The
truth of the matter is he was neither. He was
opposed to war, and is the author of what little
peace philosophy we have. He was as far from
such historic characters as Alexander, Caesar,
Charlemagne, Napoleon and Wilhelm as it was
possible for a perfect human being to be. He
was in no sense a militarist nor a physical giant.
Neither was he a pale, pallid anaemic, nor a
dreamy mystic. On the physical side Jesus was
a real man. No one can study the story of his
career as given in the gospels, without feeling
that he is standing in the presence of One, normal and natural in his physical being, with a
body, capable of being the temple of God.

He had wisdom. The leaders of his day were
astonished at his knowledge of books and the
things of culture. Jesus handled some of the
pre-conceived notions in the realm of the intellectual with divine recklessness, but he had
grasped the essentials in the wisdom of the
books and schools. He read accurately the
great book of nature. The birds, lilies, rivers,
lakes, mountains, trees, vineyards, flocks, folds
and the fields were chapters in that great book
of life whose message tells of God. When Luke
says he increased in wisdom, we are prepared
to follow him through life, and we find that he

learned as he passed along. He grew in the consciousness of God, and humanity, as the expression of God, and had at last that wisdom so far beyond books and schools that the makers of books and the founders of schools must look to him for inspiration and guidance.

He had the social qualities of life in the very beginning of his career, and grew in this respect. He was not what we call "sociable." But he was social. He regarded the humblest man as a part of the economy of God. He found fine expressions of humanity, but a revelation of God in fishermen and tax-gatherers; publicans and sinners; wayfarers and outcasts. He was the son of a carpenter, but had in his veins the blood of kings. He impressed all humanity everywhere. Those who did not love him feared him. As he approached the end of his earthly career it was the realization on the part of the established social and political order that a new type of humanity had arisen that made them lead him to the judgment hall and out to Calvary. Jesus is the only character of history, who was able to sum up in his being the social longings of all the past and anticipate the perfection of these longings in the tomorrow of the world.

He grew in favor with God. It is a little difficult for us to understand this with our pre-conceived notions of his messiahship. It is not difficult, however, when we realize God's method of bringing his Messiah into this world. He could have created him instantaneously, or could have dropped him out of heaven as a full-grown man. Growth is the law of the universe. And so the Messiah grew. Jesus advanced in the knowledge of God until he could say he who has seen me has seen the Father. It seems a long journey from the cradle in Bethlehem to the throne of the ages; but however long the journey, it was one of a growing consciousness of God, and of the value of the soul.

Before we go on to an application of the two fundamental principles of modern education as interpreted by some of the great prophets of the same, it will be well for us to pause long enough to emphasize again two things: First, Christianity furnished the model child for the race whose development was normal; second, it also furnishes the Model Teacher, who out of his consciousness of God and self, taught the final message of life. At last all true education is Christian. Only that which is distinctively Christian can be called education.

PROPHETS OF EDUCATION

Let us consider again the statements by different leading educators as to what constitutes modern education. Spencer, "To prepare us for a complete living." Butler, "A gradual adjustment to the spiritual possession of the race." Coe, "An effort to assist immature persons to realize themselves and their destiny as persons." Drawbridge, "Taking one living idea at a time from one's mind and planting it so that it will grow in the mind of another." Du Bois, "Teaching is enabling another to restate the truth in terms of one's own life." Colonel Roosevelt, "Education is the art of human adjustment; doing the right thing at the right time."

Putting all these together we have a fairly clear conception of modern education by modern educators. No one would be satisfied to take a single one of the six and make it final. But together they make a good summary of education. Based upon these there are at least six things included in the educational program.

1. Education is the process by which we are prepared for complete living, for life. It is more than intellectual development. It includes the entire round of being. How remarkably this principle reminds us of the statement of Jesus about the life more abundant. He came that we might have life, and that abundantly.

2. Education is the gradual adjustment of the individual to the spiritual possessions of the

race. It is social and universally spiritual. All that has transpired anywhere and everywhere, contributes to the education of the modern man. All that every great teacher has taught becomes mine. My education grows as I come to have a gradual adjustment to the spiritual possessions of the entire race. This, too, is Christian. From the standpoint of Jesus and Paul, "All things are ours."

3. Education is helping the immature person to realize himself and his eternal destiny. School-days are not over when we come to the end of this earthly career. We are merely prepared to pass to the next stage. One's education never really begins until he is able to think of himself as a part of an eternal order, and his education progresses as he becomes conscious of his eternal relationship. This reminds us of the teaching of Jesus, and especially the Father's house of many mansions; the intercessory prayer in the seventeenth chapter of John; and his sublime utterance, "I am the resurrection and the life."

4. Education is planting a living thought from your own mind in the mind of another that it may grow in the formation of character. True education is dynamic, not static; it is vital, not mechanical; it is growing, not stationary. This is most certainly a Christian conception

for Jesus stated that the Kingdom of Heaven was like a sower going forth to sow. The word is the seed of the Kingdom.

5. Education is that process by which we are taught to restate truth in terms of our own experience and life. An idea is never mine until I can state it anew out of my own experience. We begin to reach this climax of education as we approach this ideal. This, too, is perfectly Christian. With Christ the individual is supreme; the soul is the only human reality worth while; and man never comes to the consciousness of his highest estate until "Christ is formed within him the hope of glory." In other words truth and love must become incarnate. We must know the truth before the truth can make us free.

6. Education is the fine art of being able to do the right thing at the right time. It is not sufficient to learn how men of another age acted. We might do this and fail. Education consists of taking the wisdom of the world and utilizing it in being at home, and of service in God's big world. This reminds us of the parable of the two builders: the man who heard and acted built his house upon a rock. Here education and religion meet. The blessing is not to him who says, "Lord, Lord," but to him who does the will of the Lord.

A number of years ago I heard a noted educator say that in the final analysis the preacher and the teacher have the same task. It seems to me this is true. If the terms of the teacher are translated into the terms of the preacher, and vice versa, we shall find that the objective is the same. The joint task of teaching and preaching is the nurture of souls in the image of God that they may be at home in the universe, the Father's house of many mansions.

EVANGELISTIC PREACHING

Preach the word.—2 Timothy 4:2.

I am not an evangelist but it is with regret that I am compelled to admit it. The first passion that stirred within me after becoming a member of the church was to be an evangelist. I would rather now go to some church anxious to win souls for Christ and spend a month in that holy task than to take any vacation I can imagine. You are not interested, however, in my personal desire and feelings. But I would like for you to know, you winners of men, that I share your holy zeal and am deeply and vitally interested in your splendid task.

The only justification I can make for my manner of life is that it seems as essential to be a secretary and promoter of the enterprizes of the Kingdom of God through this method as to engage in other callings. I come to you, therefore, as a preacher and promoter, a secretary and servant of all the interests of all the people of our great movement.

The one supreme task before our brotherhood at home and abroad is the winning of souls for Jesus Christ. In the final analysis there is no such thing as home missions and foreign missions. The missionary is an evangelist and the evangelist is a missionary; and the secretary, whether he holds the humble position of leader of forces within a state or occupies a larger place in our general work, should be a promoter of all that enlarges the borders of the Kingdom of God.

There is a task more fundamental than that of outlining a series of evangelistic sermons and I shall deal with it before coming to my special theme. I wonder what this is all about. What are we trying to do? What are the aims, motives and purposes of our people today? Are we trying to add another denomination to a list altogether too long now, or do we have some greater motive than can possibly concern the most pious of denominationalists? What is our task? Have we been where we are going? Have we arrived?

The evangelist is a specialized servant of Christ. In my judgment he comes as near representing all the interests of the church as any other servant of our Lord. You will pardon me for saying that I am not uttering this sentiment merely because this is an evangelistic institute. I believe it and am glad to give honor to whom honor is due.

The evangelist comes to a church for a short period to arouse, inspire, instruct, direct, enlarge and emotionalize the entire program of the local church. He cannot, therefore, be merely the manipulator of an adding machine. He ought to be interested in numbers. He is no evangelist who glories in the fewness of his recruits. But the man who has his eye only on the adding machine, or who thinks exclusively of numbers, will miss the mark.

With the idea in mind, therefore, that the task of the evangelist is such as I have outlined I would like to offer a number of suggestions as to the type of preaching he ought to do in a series of meetings.

1. The evangelist should establish a proper point of contact between himself and the local church. A sermon or so on the historic position of the Disciples of Christ and our relation to the religious world in general, is in order as an introductory to a series of evangelistic meetings. We are ready, at once, to say that this is a sectarian appeal, partisan prejudice and denominational loyalty. I am ignoring that technical discussion as to whether or not we are a denomination. But I shall have to say with the greatest plainness I know how to use, that if a man is going to have a series of meetings for and with and through a local church the first thing for him to do is to establish a point of contact with that congregation and with the body of which it is a part.

Nothing will help a meeting more in its opening stages than for the people to feel, that the man who has come among them to hold a meeting connects them properly with the great brotherhood and that he is capable of introducing them as a Christian gentleman and a believer in their message to their religious neighbors. A meeting cannot succeed in an atmosphere of suspicion and uncertainty.

2. We have been accustomed to say that the first thing for an evangelist to do is to "trim the church." It has been the rather common practice for the evangelist to spend a week or more of his valuable time "dressing up the church." Personally, I have serious misgivings as to the advisability of this. Some of our churches have had an unbroken history in communities for a hundred years. They have certain set forms and social ceremonies, peculiarities and idiosyncrasies, that cannot be changed "in a moment, in the twinkling of an eye," nor by a series of evangelistic meetings running through a month or six weeks.

There are gross wrongs in the church that ought to be condemned; but ordinarily it is better to preach a few sermons on a big constructive program for the local church, and make an honest effort to "overcome evil with good" than to try to rally the community by getting everybody in the church mad at the evangelist. After establishing this point of contact historically and locally with the church the evangelist can with great profit to the cause and especially his meeting preach a few sermons on what the church ought to be in the community. We have learned to say that a hint to the wise is sufficient, and a constructive outline of church policy presented in a few sermons will do more good than all the drastic criticism that could be given in a month. It takes more courage to do this than it does to start a row.

3. The evangelist must get the attention of the community. Some would say that he must get the attention first. But whether he gets it before he establishes his fellowship with the church or afterward he must have the attention of the community. Here is where some of us fall down. There is a certain round of sermons on theater-going, card-playing and dancing. And many times the community is regaled with a lot of material bordering on the obscene and profane to get the crowd. In these days it is frequently the case that we include some criticisms concerning the costumes that the women wear, or do not wear, and thus add to our trinity of wicked amusements.

Now, I am a believer in sermons against these social evils and follies. But it is bad taste to spend so much time on them when there are politicians in the church who buy elections; and big brethren who gamble on the Board of Trade; and landlords who are unjust to their tenants; and merchants who are shady in their business and so on. Instead of specializing on dancing, the evangelist can get the attention of the community by delivering a big social message that makes the community feel a new day has dawned, and that at last the church has made up its mind to honestly strive to apply religion to everyday life. These social follies will pass away when humanity gets interested in something better.

If we can only come to see it, the most sensational thing possible is giving the people of a community to understand that we are taking our religion seriously; and that a series of evangelistic meetings is now in progress at the Christian church, the primary aim of which is to teach the people that religion is practical and that it ought to be lived. The evangelist can afford, therefore, to have a few sermons on what we call the social message. In fact he cannot afford to be without them.

After he denounces the social sins of the community, he can lead the people very easily to understand the necessity of a larger application of the principles of the gospel to the work-a-day world. In other words he ought to pray for the coming of the Kingdom and preach that he may help its advance.

4. The suggestions I am now offering have reference to the holding of evangelistic meetings in communities in which our cause is somewhat established. In such places it is not necessary any longer to conduct a thirty-day argumentation to prove the truthfulness of our plea. In pioneer days the sermons were, and in pioneer communities the majority should probably be, on what we call first principles. Such meetings ought to be conducted primarily for the impartation of information on all these great themes of the Bible. But in the more established communites it is not necessary to conduct a prolonged argumentation. The evangelist should remember that he is holding a gospel meeting and not conducting a school of logic.

I am not saying that the time has come to cease preaching on such themes as: "The Two Covenants"; "The Laws of Hearts and Stones"; "Moses and Christ"; "The Right Division of the Word"; "The Establishment of the Church", etc. Every series of evangelistic meetings should have ringing messages on these and kindred topics, but one week out of four devoted to special themes of this kind is probably sufficient for purposes of indoctrinating the people. These may be preached continuously or probably to a better advantage scattered through the meeting.

5. The evangelist has not been called to the church to deliver a Christian apologetic. No man can establish the truthfulness of Christianity in a series of evangelistic meetings; and to convert such a meeting into a forum to prove the existence of God, the inspiration of the Scriptures, the divinity of Christ, or the reality of miracles is to wander from the path. Themes of this character should be presented but they should be declared rather than defended, proclaimed rather than proved. They should be presented with the confidence that inspires faith. To divert a revival meeting into a technical discussion of the existence of God or the reality of miracles is to fail in the accomplishment of its purpose.

If the evangelist finds a community in which that is needed, the need should be met, not in a regular evangelistic campaign, but in a course of lectures or studies intended to go to the very seat of the intellectual difficulty. The evangelist can do more good in declaring the whole counsel of God than in trying to prove the truthfulness of his message. There are only a few people in every community who are intellectually "at sea." It is folly to convert an entire community into a debating society in order to handle such a small minority.

6. I should say that the larger part of the evangelistic message of today should be an appeal to follow Christ. A great variety of sermons is possible along this line. I am inclined to think after looking over a list of considerably more than three hundred sermon topics for meetings, collected from pastors and evangelists, that a great part of our preaching is of that character.

The purpose of the evangelist is primarily to secure recruits. Let us admit that and it will help us to understand some other problems. The things I have mentioned thus far are for the purpose of establishing a point of contact with the church, of securing the attention of the community, of inspiring faith in the triumphant certainties of our religion and the impartation of a sufficient amount of knowledge to enable the people to know what to do.

But the evangelist is to make an appeal. If he fails to secure recruits he is disappointed and he is justified in being disappointed. This being the case more than one-half of all the preaching of a series of meetings should be devoted to definite personal appeals to the people to hear Jesus Christ, to believe in him implicitly, to confess his name before the community,

to obey him fully, to love him devotedly and to
work with him for the salvation of the race.

This appeal will have to be varied. It will
be a call to children and to adults, to the let-
tered and unlettered, to the rich and the poor.
It will be an appeal to all. With some of us
exhortation is a lost art and I presume the reason is that in many cases it has degenerated
into a meaningless sentimentalism and in other
cases purely a legalistic demand. There is a
place for exhortation just as there is a climax
in the drama, a peroration in the lecture, and a
grand finale in the music. There should be
application, appeal and an exhortation in the
sermon. The goal is action. It can be secured
by appeal.

7. The evangelist is called upon to deliver
numerous special addresses and he ought to be
fully prepared to meet these issues. He will
frequently be invited to address the high school,
and if ever a preacher is put to a real test it is
when he is called upon to go before a group of
young Americans, who are studying according
to the curriculum of the modern high school, college or university. It is not my province to
outline the address for the preacher on this
occasion, but it will have to be in the light of
learning and ought to deal with the funda-

mental issues of culture and character and find its highest appeal in the call of Christ.

There will be many openings also for addresses before women's clubs and literary groups and here is a big opportunity to show the superiority of the Bible as literature. Such themes as "The Poetry of the Bible"; "Job, the Model Drama"; and "Bible Sermons and Songs"; would be suitable for such meetings.

It may require a little tact but it will not be difficult to get invitations for the evangelist to address the Chamber of Commerce, associations of business men, the Rotary Club and other groups of that character. Here an evangelist will find a fruitful field for the presentation of business and religion.

In appeals to lodges and fraternal organizations of many kinds the real fraternalism of Christianity may be presented. I believe in addresses to men only and women only. In addressing men there are many problems that can be left to the physician better than they can be handled by the preacher. But no evangelist should miss an opportunity to present some such theme as this, "A Man's Religion," and through this make an appeal to the strongest and sturdiest within man for the service of our Lord.

Women read enough and criticize themselves enough about their dress. I doubt the advisability of the evangelist prostituting a holy service, designed to call women to the higher life, to a discussion of the fashion plate and semi-nude women.

In all of these addresses to schools, clubs, associations, lodges or what not, the one supreme task of the evangelist should be to popularize religion and make men and women everywhere see that the holiest pursuit of this busy life is to worship God and serve men in Jesus Christ our Lord.

8. The evangelist will come at last to think of the closing days of his campaign. I can understand with what singleness of aim he comes to the end of a revival meeting. This is one part of a meeting that would scare me if I were a regular evangelist.

The meeting should leave the church stronger numerically and spiritually. It should leave it with a better program for the future, a stronger hold upon the community and with more resources of every kind at its command. The revival meeting that at the end merely hands a list of names to the church clerk is a failure and the longer the list the bigger the failure.

Our evangelists see this more clearly than the secretary or the pastor does and I need not devote much time in exhortation to you men of the front rank. But I believe you will be glad to have me say in your behalf that the revival meeting ought to strengthen the educational facilities and plans of the church; it ought to increase the number of tithers and put stewardship before the people as never before; it ought to broaden the missionary vision of the church and increase giving to the cause of the Kingdom; it ought to deepen the spiritual life of the entire fellowship and leave the church an aggressive evangelistic agency and missionary dynamo.

It might be a good thing if the church does not have an educational program to help the pastor organize his church as an educational unity in religion. It might be well also to help the church put on the Every Member Canvass and make it thorough. If the church needs a new building, the revival meeting should inspire the brethren to begin plans at once for the erection of a proper structure. If the pastor is living in a borrowed or hired house, a parsonage might result from the meeting.

In other words, if the church before the meeting in its financial, social, educational and religious life has been on the basis of fifty per cent, a single revival meeting properly managed and conducted in the name of the Lord ought to increase the percentage to at least eighty.

SOME TOPICS FOR EVANGELISTIC SERMONS

Some time ago it occurred to me that it would be helpful to us to have a list of themes used by our preachers in evangelistic campaigns. I wrote a number of men who have been successful in various types of evangelism and secured the list I am submitting herewith. It would be better if we had the texts that suggest the topics, but they were not given, so I will give the topics without them.

A Full Grown Man
How Much Owest Thou
God and My Brother
Stewardship
Lifting Up the Son of Man
Rebuilding the Spiritual Walls of Jerusalem
The Sin of Division
Sowing and Reaping
The Basis of Unity
The A B C's of Obedience and Service
A Glorious Church
The Power of the Word
The Place of Religion in Life
If Not Christ, Then What
The Faith That Saves
The Summer Is Ended, the Harvest Is Past

Follow Thou Me
Who Is Jesus
Pilate or Christ, Which
The Authority of the Church
Baptism
Life Eternal
The Book Our Mothers Read
The Law of Pardon
The Conversion of a Statesman
The Trembling Judge
Choose Ye This Day
Finding God
What Is a Christian
The Last Judgment
Repent or Perish
Christ's Confidence in Men
Rejecting Christ
The Church—Christ's Body
Christ Walking with His Own
Why I Am What I Am
The Other Fellow
Leprosy and Sin
Avenues to Hell
What Is Your Destination
Finding a Man
The Church as Jesus Saw It
The Living Stones
What Is Salvation
The Evidences of Salvation

The Power of the Human Will
Can a Man Find God
The Upper Room
His Last Night
The Changeless God in a Changing World
The Humanity of Jesus
The Atoning Blood
If Jesus Were Here
The New Testament Church
The Master Is Here and Calleth for Thee
Removing the Stumbling Stones
Letting Your Light Shine
God's Eternal Purpose
Punishment for Sin
Why Study the Bible
The Manliness of Jesus
The True Basis of Hope
The Oneness of the People of God
The Enlargement of Life
How May We Know God
The Two Covenants
True Repentance
The Profit of Godliness
Does Man Need a Savior
Risen with Christ
The Door
The Great Invitation
The Divinity of Christ
Repentance

The Church
Great Motives
The Hidden and Revealed
The Inerrant Creed
Saved from Suicide
Immortality of Influence
Suffering and Glory
The Gospel of Service
Losing and Finding
The Heavenly Home
We Would See Jesus
The Unchanging Christ
The Greatness of Service
Christ in Prophecy
Drifting
The Books Opened
Christ Enthroned
The Greatest Sin
In Christ
The Faith That Saves
The Supervising Architect
The Master Builders
The Means of Salvation
The Basis for World Evangelism
The Universal Prayer
Seeing the Invisible
The Saving Power of Christ
The Life More Abundant
A Divine Benediction

How the Worst Sinner Was Saved
Transplanted Christians
Nine Men Who Forgot Something
When Jesus Comes
The Purpose of the Holy Scriptures
A Sermon in Dust
When Iron Floats
Not by Water Only
The Simplicity of Conversion
Four Essentials to Real Church Life
The Exaltation of Christ
Back to Christ
The Supreme Question
Visions and Dreams
The Witness of the Spirit
What Will You Do with Jesus
The New Birth and the Christian Life
The Other Side
What Time Is It
How Do We Get Religion
The Divine Nature of Christ
Two Ways
The Samaritan Woman
The Prodigal Son
Facts About Sin
What It Means to Be a Christian
Now Is the Accepted Time
God Seeking Men
The Value of the Soul

The Journey of Life
Unsearchable Riches
When All Else Fails
The Vision That Saves
The Tragedy of What Might Have Been
Pen Knife Religion
Fatal Mistakes
Our Plea and Program
Kicking Against the Goads
How Do Men Become Believers
The Appeal of the Cross
The Joy of Finding the Lost
What Think Ye of Christ
Why Did Christ Die
The Divine Call
Seeking the Lord
The Path of Life
The Garden of the Soul
Where God Meets Man
The Home of the Redeemed
Jesus and the Masses
Religion in Common Life
Where Thy Treasure Is
God's Part in Man's Conversion
Man's Part in God's Redemption
The Sweetest Story Ever Told
The Parting of the Ways
Is Baptism Necessary
Convinced But Not Converted

Behold He Prayeth
Rightly Dividing the Word
The Law Fulfilled
Weighed in the Balances
One Thing Lacking
Fifteen Things That Save
Faith in Salvation
A Wise Choice
Pardon
Heaven
The Infallibly Safe Way
The Dividing Line
Gilt-Edged Security
A Poor Bargain
Are the Scriptures Sufficient
The Great Confession
What Must I Do to Be Saved
What Must I Do to Be Lost
The Christian Church
Neglect and Its Consequences
Excuses
Elements of a Successful Revival
Man Seeking God
Does the World Need a Savior
The Savior the World Needs
The Divine Appointment
Transforming Power
Burning Questions
Set Thine House in Order

The Age-Long Mission of the Church
Harden Not Your Hearts
The Bible Estimate of Man
The Obedience of Faith
Giving the More Earnest Heed
The Greatness of Christ
The Power of a Name
Christ Seeking the Lost
The Lost Sheep
The Lost Boy
The Cleansing Fountain
What Is Your Life
A Study in Profit and Loss
Gates of Eden
The Empty House
New Testament Conversion
The Lordship of Jesus
Living Life Over Again
The Credentials of Jesus
What Is Your Life
The Value of a Soul
Whosoever Will
A Successful Inquirer
The Bible a Reasonable Book
The Bread of Life
The Sin of Omission
The Eternal Christ
Christ in the World
Overcoming Through Faith

The Reasonableness of the Gospel
The Basis of Our Hope
The Finality of the Gospel
Heartfelt Religion
The Unpardonable Sin
The Laborer and the Harvest
Sin and Its Wages
The Power of Choice
Christ in the Human Heart
Doubts and Objections
Paradise Lost and Regained

TWO KINDS OF EVANGELISM

Go ye . . . . make disciples . . . . baptizing them
. . . . teaching them to observe all things.—Matthew 28:
19, 20.

I am not a specialist in evangelism, but I have a deep and abiding interest in the subject. A preacher without an evangel is really a man without a job. When the time comes that we lose interest in the evangelistic activity of the church, we have come to the end of the day. And it is by no means a perfect day.

Evangelism is the name we give the effort made to win men for Christ and his Kingdom. Evangelism is Kingdom extension. We may classify our evangelism, but in the final analysis it is one. Technically, there is only one kind of evangelism; but for practical purposes I am to speak of two. Sometimes a subject is cleared up by an analysis previous to the discussion. I hope it may be so in this case.

One who is somewhat expert in the matter of evangelism has divided the subject into a number of sub-heads: professional, personal, educational, social, architectural, financial and spiritual. For my purposes in this address this analysis is not necessary. The two kinds of

101

evangelism I have in mind are found in either of these I have just mentioned. They must be present in every program of evangelism.

The church will live and enlarge her borders just in proportion as she is evangelistic. She must go on or go out. A stationary engine may be of value, but a stationary Christian is an impossibility. There is no way to evade responsibility. To be a Christian one must be evangelistic. Christ said, "Come" that he might say, "Go." We are invited that we may be commanded. It is do or die; it is extension or extinction. The unevangelistic church is already dead. It is doubtful whether it is the undertaker or the evangelist who is needed. It may be that a funeral is more timely than a revival. Before you offer to administer extreme unction try to hold a revival.

So it is quite clear that there are two types of evangelism. This is seen in the time we set for our meetings. We are demanding two seasons for the work of extension. A distinct type of meeting is needed for the autumn. Then there is an urgent call for the pre-Easter campaign. It is quite evident that you cannot hold the same kind of meeting in the fall that you hold at the Easter season. The calendar itself is dividing our evangelism into two types.

Their Names

For the sake of better terms we call these two kinds of evangelism the cultural and the conversional. These are only relative terms, for all evangelism must be both cultural and conversional. The name is derived from the maximum emphasis.

We are producing quite an extensive evangelistic literature. There are four books in my library that represent the two types. In one group I have these two volumes, *Twice-Born Men* and *Those Who Have Come Back*. In the other group I have *Educational Evangelism* and *Christian Nurture*. The first shows the need of an extra pedagogical force. The second tells quite fully how to build up the church through her educational functions. Our libraries contain numerous volumes on the Bible school and other organizations of the church as evangelistic agencies. Then we have many volumes similar to *Twice-Born Men* and *Those Who Have Come Back*. The temperament of the minister or evangelist may incline him one way or the other. But the man who is one-sided will not make the success he should in building up the church. We need both methods.

The cultural and conversional are ever present. It is a mere matter of which is in the ascendancy. *Twice-Born Men* may not be pedagogical and educational evangelism may be lacking in the emotional element. But for the evangelism of our day, it is absolutely necessary that we understand both and the ideals of each. Let us look at them.

THE CULTURAL

Cultural or educational evangelism relies upon the teaching functions of the church for its success. The process may be slow and the results may not be subject to tabulation. The adding machine may be of little value in this method of Kingdom-building. But the efforts are just as essential as if they could be reduced to arithmetic. Cultural evangelism presupposes the native religious nature of man. It assumes that he is "incurably religious." It rejects the doctrine of inborn sin, denies the necessity of wild-oats sowing and proclaims the possibility of normal religious development.

The advocate of educational evangelism may not go as far as Horace Bushnell and maintain that a child ought to grow up religiously, and never know that it had ever been anything else but a religious being. But he does believe that the child can and ought to turn to God naturally. This type of evangelism draws much inspiration from the story of the development of Jesus. Luke says that Jesus increased physically, mentally, socially and spiritually. I am not maintaining that it is possible for a human being to attain unto the perfection of Jesus; but we are admonished to grow until we come "to the measure of the stature of the fullness of Jesus Christ." The fact that Jesus developed normally along the four lines indicated encourages me to believe that there are unrealized possibilities in all children. I once heard a noted evangelist say, "Let go and let God." I believe this is a fair statement of the case. Give the child a chance and he will turn to God naturally. The purpose of the church should be to so train the child that it will come to its consciousness of God by the natural and normal unfoldment of life. This is educational evangelism. We are to save from sinning as well as from sin.

The Disciples are well prepared for leadership in this type of work. Alexander Campbell was a teacher of religion. If he were alive today he would hardly be regarded as a revivalist. He did not hold many meetings of length. But he was a teacher of religion. He started a religious paper. He conducted the *Christian Baptist* for seven years, and discontinued it only that he might start another paper with a somewhat different spirit. Why did Alexander Campbell start a religious paper? Because he

believed in the power of the printed page in
the propagation of the Kingdom of God. He
founded Bethany College, a Christian school,
educationally the mother of us all. He made
the Bible a textbook in that college. Why did
he start a college? Because he believed the
cause he was advocating would grow—just in
proportion as he could train preachers and
teachers to carry it to the ends of the earth.
Yes, Alexander Campbell was a teacher rather
than a revivalist. He did not make it the rule
of his life to hold protracted meetings. This is
no criticism on evangelism or revivalism. Mr.
Campbell was a great friend of Walter Scott
and Barton W. Stone, two wonderful evangelists. But Mr. Campbell so far as his own life
was concerned placed the emphasis upon education in religion.

As a people we started right, but we have
lost much time and wasted a great deal of
energy. We ought to have become leaders in
religious education. We have been theoretically correct for more than a hundred years, but
practically we have not delivered the goods.

Have we not emphasized the fact that the
disciples were called Christians first in Antioch?
It was a group of learners who were called
Christians. The Antioch church was one in
which the membership was enrolled as learners

in the School of Jesus. And because of this the disciples were called Christians. Only disciples of Christ ought to be called Christians.

From the beginning of our movement we have said two things: First, no man can become a Christian until he learns how; second, no man can become a better Christian except as he learns the way of the Lord more perfectly. I therefore draw the conclusion that the church is, and of right ought to be, an educational institution, dedicated to the task of teaching young and old out of Christ to know him; and of building up the membership of the body of Christ in the knowledge of our Lord. Cultural or educational evangelism must have a large place in our program of activities. We must teach as well as preach.

THE CONVERSIONAL

By conversional evangelism I mean that type of evangelism that demands a turning away from sin and to the Lord. We have talked quite a bit about adult or alien evangelism, but I prefer the term "conversional." We seek to convert, to turn, to change, to renew, to bring back, to reform and transform. For the world in sin, there is but one message, Turn from sin and unto the Lord.

Much of the evangelism of the New Testament is of this type. This was true of Peter on Pentecost; Stephen in his defense; Philip in Samaria; Peter before Cornelius; and Paul everywhere. The appeal was to adults. But it is not difficult to see why. The church was a new institution. It was established in a world that needed converting. Its first appeal was to the men and women of the Jewish nation. Its first appeal to Gentiles was also to adults. We should not draw a conclusion that would make us less interested in the Bible school; but it is a fact that this appeal to adults must still be made and with greater emphasis than ever.

I am told that what I have called conversional evangelism is psychologically irrational. This may be so. I am not up on the latest in psychology. But if it is irrational, it is because man in sin is irrational. I prefer, however, to change the criticism and admit that it is abnormal. The sinner is abnormal and it will take an abnormal method to reach him. He must be jolted. He must be dynamited. He is dead and must come to life. Those who believe in the resurrection of the dead will have confidence in this type of evangelism. Dynamite may be a little more explosive than what we call "the dynamic"; but there are some mental, moral and social conditions that cannot possibly be loosened up with anything less than dynamite.

What we want is results. If it takes dynamite, let us use it. The world is here. It contains two general types of individuals: those who can be trained in the nurture and admonition of the Lord and those who must be brought back from ways of sin and shown the necessity of living life over again. So long as we have the two types of people we will need the two methods of evangelism.

We need the Quaker with his quiet serene soul and his well-poised temperament. But in some communities we need the earthquaker before the Quaker can operate. There are men and women in every community who must be shocked. A pink-tea party spirit will not meet the issue. It is still necessary to storm the fort. This may not be ideal, but it is necessary. Says one, this is opportunism. I am willing to be written down as an "opportunist" provided I can get results.

Again, our evangelism must meet man as he is. I may again run counter to certain conclusions of modern psychology. We are not as certain today as we once were of the analysis of man into intellect, sensibility and will. But we have not outgrown the fact that man can know, feel and do. Our evangelism must meet him in these three capacities. Man must know the truth, feel the urgency of divine love, and obey the will of God. The evangelist should impart a sufficient amount of information to make clear the matter of becoming a Christian. Then he should make the strongest emotional appeal within his power. And in his climax he should drive hard to get action. The message must fit the man. It must fit his intellect, his emotional nature and his will-power. The gospel, like the Sabbath, is for man and not man for the gospel.

Evangelists must hit sin hard. The community must be made to face itself. This requires more than one big sermon on that famous triumvirate—card-playing, theater-going and dancing. We are not advocating that evangelists should let up in their preaching against these things. But the man who feels he has discharged his social responsibility to the community when he has condemned these three evils is very badly mistaken.

An evangelistic campaign of the right kind will arouse the community against dishonesty in business, crookedness in politics, laxness in the public school, immorality in the community and every other form of vice. It will criticize women for gambling on Thursday afternoon and it will condemn the leading brethren for gambling on the Board of Trade and for robbing widows and orphans.

Yes, an evangelistic campaign is an attack upon the conscience of the community, both individual and social. The evangelist must ever bear in mind that the ideal is not reached until the saved man is part of a redeemed society. Science, philosophy and religion agree that man in his redemption must be considered in relation to his social environment.

Evangelistic sermons ought to be scriptural. We could easily do without many of the stories we tell and much of the personal experience we relate. The human experiences of the Bible are better than any we have had and they will go further with the people. Evangelists ought to use these instead of so many personal reminiscences and crude stories. We ought to preach a good deal on first principles, but it will help the revival meeting very much if there are several sermons on second principles. Many of our old sermons could be rewritten with profit to ourselves and an advantage to the first principles themselves. Too many revival meetings are conducted with time-worn sermons and stereotyped method. We might at least change thirdly and firstly or it wouldn't hurt once in a while to preach without the ordinary mathematical sermonic formularies. The fact of the business is with most of our sermons on first principles, one can safely retire so far as think-

ing is concerned after he hears the opening
statement or reads the first paragraph.

Have you ever taken an inventory of the sermonic literature you have produced? If you
have not, then you have a deeply humiliating
experience before you. We have a revised version of the New Testament and then we have
the American edition of the revised version.
Brethren, why not have an American edition
of the revised version of some of our sermons
on first principles?

Their Operations

The church ought to be an educational unit
in religion. Every agency in the church and
of the church ought to be constituted for the
one purpose of teaching the religion of Christ.
The Bible school has no other mission. Neither
has the Christian Endeavor Society. The Missionary Society has lost its way if it fails to
realize this. The Official Board of the church
could spend less time in the numerous efforts
to save money and use it profitably in forming
plans for the propagation of the gospel in the
community. A church board that will spend
its days in planning evangelistic campaigns and
work for the general upbuilding of the church
will find the money problem an easy one to
solve. If the church will dedicate herself unre-

servedly and with enthusiasm to the ministry of the Word, the money will come into the treasury of the Lord sufficient for the needs of the work.

There should be seasons for enlistment. Four have been mentioned as the most favorable. (1) *Christmas*.—No better time could be found to present the cause of Christ to the childhood of the church than at that glad season when we celebrate his birthday. (2) *Easter*.—The resurrection morning will always have its appeal. It proves that Christianity is a religion of life. What a wonderful opportunity for the life-call. (3) *Children's Day.*—This has been used most advantageously for the development of a missionary conscience. It is a good time to bring the missionary appeal home to each child personally in the dedication of life as well as money. (4) *School opening*.—The opening of the public schools in America is a high tide in the life of our people. Why not make it a good day for enrollment in the Bible school and enlistment in the school of Christ—the church. Other seasons will occur to you but these four will make a splendid program for any church.

But, in addition to seasonal evangelism when enlistment and recruitment are the great issues, I wish to make an ardent appeal for an annual evangelistic campaign, whose chief aim shall be to challenge the intellect, the heart, the will, the conscience and the social life of the community. This must be a real campaign not for the purpose of manipulating an adding machine, but for the purpose of bringing religion with all the power at the command of the church to the attention of the community. Numbers will come and they ought to come. God has a book of "numbers" in the Bible. But the end is character.

With a program of religious education that permeates the entire church, culminating in an enlistment service and with an evangelistic campaign of the conversional type, as outlined above, the church is prepared to meet her real problem and serve the religious needs of the community. Two kinds of evangelism, cultural and conversional. We need both kinds.

THE PROGRAM OF EVANGELISM

And ye shall be my witnesses both in Jerusalem, and in all Judea and Samaria, and unto the uttermost part of the earth.—Acts 1:8.

It is no longer necessary to argue in behalf of evangelism. We have come to see that this is merely the name we apply to the efforts of the church to extend her borders and make effective the message of Christ. The words "evangel" and "gospel" mean about the same thing. Evangel is a message of hope. The gospel is good news. Evangelism is the program of the church for bringing this hope to the world and announcing the good news.

In thinking of the program of evangelism I have tried to look at it from several different angles. This analysis is by no means exhaustive and some of the sub-titles might be changed in the interest of clearness and accuracy. But for my own purposes of thinking through my plan of work as a minister of Christ, I like to outline the program of evangelism in this way.

1. *Personal evangelism.*—The thing that distinguishes Christianity from other religions and philosophies of life is that it exalts personality and makes the individual outstanding. Chris-

tianity is a religion of personalities: God, Christ, Man.

Naturally a religion that exalts the personal element and makes the individual supreme would place a high value upon reaching one person by another. In the final analysis, therefore, all evangelism is personal.

The story of Jesus as revealed in the fourfold gospel is certainly attractive. He stands out as the mighty personage who says, "Come unto me," and then proclaims, "Go ye into all the world." His message is largely one of verbs: come, go, ask, seek, knock, love, serve, teach, and preach. Jesus was a personal worker. He talked to the masses but had his greatest success when speaking to individuals. His strongest appeals were to the few men by the Sea of Galilee, to Matthew the publican at his task, to the woman at Jacob's well, to Nicodemus about the new birth and to the rich young ruler. If ever there was a non-conformist in this world Jesus of Nazareth was one. It is said of him that he went about doing good. It was not doing good in the abstract, but in personal conversations and acts of kindness.

The Book of Acts is the only authentic history we have of the activities of the early church immediately following the resurrection of our Lord. While there are some great group meetings, such as the one on Pentecost and a few days later, and some great revivals, such as the one in Samaria conducted by Philip, we find the most charming incidents in the Acts to be the conversion of the Ethiopian statesman, the Philippian jailer, and Cornelius, the centurion.

The New Testament reveals the personal appeal of Christ to individual men and women and it is clear that his church grew as its members became effective in personal work. Personal evangelism is the basis of Christian activity.

2. *Educational evangelism.*—Many figures are used in the New Testament to set forth the fellowship of those who love Christ and work with him. A study of these is interesting indeed. There is no place that I can recall where the church is called a school, but the followers of Christ are repeatedly called disciples and he is introduced to us time and again as a Teacher. The most fundamental characteristic of Christianity is its teaching function.

It is the only religion that relies absolutely upon teaching truth for its conquest in the lives of men. Many times we are mistaken with regard to the real Christian message and we miss the way in methods of propaganda. We imitate Buddhists with our dreams, Confucians with our ethical teaching, and Mohammedans when we take the sword; but the real Christian knows that Christ will come to this world only as men learn the truth.

Great advancement has been made in recent years in the matter of Christian education. But the basis of it is found in the New Testament. Our own people have from the very beginning called themselves disciples of Christ, learners in the school of Jesus. Mr. Campbell and those who labored with him were quite emphatic in their utterances, that no man can become a Christian until he learns how, and that we become better Christians by learning the way of the Lord more perfectly. I fear, however, this fundamental theory of religious education has become a dogma with many of us and has been limited to learning a few first principles.

When we take ourselves seriously and begin in dead earnest to conduct the work of Christ along educational lines, we will make a real contribution to the cause of Christian education. While the Sunday school, religious literature and the Christian college are agencies of Christian education it seems to me we must go deeper than these and regard them merely as manifestations of Christian education. The basis upon which educational evangelism operates is that all of the agencies and activities of the church ought to be so organized and conducted as to enable the church to discharge its fundamental function of teaching religion.

It is no part of this paper to give an outline of this procedure. I am not dealing with the curriculum of a school nor do I propose a plan of operation. I am simply saying that we must restore the spirit of education to all the departments of church life and make the church itself an educational unit in religion. This is educational evangelism.

3. *Seasonal evangelism.*—Protestants have been afraid of the sacred days of religion because Roman Catholics have made so much of them. Many times these days are observed as ends within themselves. They become the occasion for the display of the ritual or for emphasis upon the creed. When the holy days of the church become ends within themselves, religion has become ceremonial and ceases to have the highest value.

It would be easy to multiply times and seasons or designate days for the special declaration of the gospel. I can think of at least four occasions that could be exalted to a splendid advantage.

a) Enlistment Sunday.—The public school is the most universal institution in American life. It comes as near representing all of the people all of the time as any other agency we have.

The opening of school in the autumn is a great day throughout the land. Why not make this a season for enlistment in the activities of the church? It comes immediately after vacation time and when we are thinking of enrollment in the school life of the community. I do not know that this season could be used to a very great advantage in decisions for Christ; but it is a splendid time to recast and reorganize the Sunday school and plan for larger things through the educational activities of the church. In this sense it would become one of the most useful and happy occasions of the entire year.

b) Christmas.—This is one of the two seasons that Protestants have not rejected because of Catholic endorsement. But we have not always made Christmas what it ought to be. It has become a time for the giving of material gifts. Why not make it the time for the dedication of life? What would be more fitting than for the young people to be called upon to dedicate life to Christ as they celebrate his advent into the world? The evangelistic appeal of Christmas could be made one of the strongest of the year.

c) Easter.—Easter is another season as universal as Christian activity. In the springtime, as nature puts on a new garment and as everything indicates life and activity, we have a fine opportunity to present the call of Christ. Pre-Easter revivals have grown until they have become a big feature in the program of the church, but we can enlarge upon this and become still more effective.

d) Children's Day.—Children's Day has a place in the life of the church that will probably make it abiding. This day has been the vehicle for the impartation of missionary information and probably more people have been stirred deeply by the appeals of Children's Day in the interest of foreign missions than in any other way. Has not the time come when we can use this for the dedication of life as we have used it for the impartation of missionary information?

I was tempted to include Pentecost, but since this comes so close to Children's Day, I am in doubt whether we ought to emphasize it as a special day for life dedication or whether it ought to be used for other purposes.

A church that has its program worked out along these lines of seasonal evangelism, making the fall an enlistment season for the Sunday school and other departments of church work; Christmas the time for the beginning of the new life; Easter an awakening time; and Children's Day the graduation period in the school of Christ—such a church will have a program of life and activity that will mean progress in the Kingdom.

4. *Architectural evangelism.*—The cathedral has been called "frozen music" and the "gospel in architecture." The time has come for a re-study of church building.

There are three ideas of religion: the ceremonial, the creedal, and the cultural. Each concept has been memorialized in architecture. Tell me the kind of church buildings an age or a country erects and I will tell you its theology.

Those who believe in the ceremonial will erect cathedrals. They may be large or small. The fundamental idea of a cathedral is that ritual is supreme and ceremony final. The priest is the manipulator of ceremonies and an actor before the altar.

The early settlers who came to this country from Europe tried to get as far from ceremonial religion as possible. They built meeting-houses. These were rectangular buildings in which the preacher, not the priest, was central. His task was to declare the whole counsel of God, to defend the faith once for all delivered unto the saints and maintain with argumentation the integrity of the creed. While the cathedral was erected for the maintenance of the ceremony, the meeting-house was built for the defense of the creed. People passed from the ceremonial to the creedal and for a long time religion was made up of these two groups. The buildings erected for the use of religion were the symbols of the respective creeds. They were cathedrals or meeting-houses.

We have come to a new day. We are thinking in terms of educational principles. Christ is the teacher; his church is a school. We desire the beauty of the cathedral and need the forum of the meeting-house; but the church that meets the demands of modern life will be a pedagogical institution. It is a place where religion may be taught to all and where there is unity in the midst of a varied educational program. The church today in erecting a building for religion thinks of it, not only as a house of worship, but a place for religious education, social activity, and Christian fellowship. Since the congregation is a unity in religious education, the building erected for its work must be constructed with this end in view.

We shall continue to admire the cathedral and in times of great stress and strain may think of the church as a forum for defending the faith; but those who do the work of Christ and extend the borders of his Kingdom will build with an eye single to the teaching of religion. This is architectural evangelism—constructing a building in such a way as to make it advantageous to the preaching of the gospel of Christ.

I have in mind a church erected some twenty-five years ago at a cost of $50,000. In its day it was a wonderful structure and was talked about in its communion far and wide. But if the brethren had undertaken to do four important things as badly as possible they could not have accomplished it more completely. The church is without a basement; it is almost impossible to hear the preacher in the Sunday school room; the baptistry is a hole in the floor; and the entire building is without ventilation. If they had put a gallery in the main auditorium the stairway would probably have led out of doors instead of to the front. It would seem that the building committee believed that the people ought to be persecuted for righteousness' sake.

I have been in church after church in which the stairway to the gallery, never occupied except in times of great enthusiasm, leads more easily out of doors than to the front.

Not only should the church be constructed for the teaching of religion, but it ought to be so arranged that the entire building could be utilized as an evangelistic agency. The church has grown in spite of its architecture. May the time come when by architectural evangelism it will become easier to get larger results.

5. *Social evangelism.*—One hesitates to use this term because it is capable of two misapprehensions. Some people never think of the social side of religion except in terms of strawberry festivals, oyster suppers, and ice cream "sociables." Others think that religion consists of back-slapping and hand-shaking. Now this is no argument against feasting functions in the church or the exercise of friendliness in the aisles of the sanctuary. But I am not thinking of these things when speaking of social evangelism.

It will help us to get this idea clearly before our minds if we remember that Christianity consists of two things, individual salvation and social redemption. It is true that Christ dealt with the individual and that in all redemptive processes the individual is first. The New Testament talks about the Kingdom of Heaven. The Kingdom of Heaven is the social expression of Christ. It is the lengthened expression of his timeless life. We are taught to pray, "Thy kingdom come." We are reminded of the fact that the kingdoms of this world will become the Kingdom of Christ. This is social evangelism —bringing in the Kingdom. God has expressed and is still expressing himself. Jesus said, "My

Father worketh hitherto and I work." Thus God is revealing himself. Nature is the material expression of God; the Bible is the literary expression of God; Christ is the human expression of God; and a redeemed humanity will be the social expression of God. The goal before the church is nothing short of the complete redemption of mankind. That will be the final chapter of the book of God.

The church is to learn the will of God; it is also to do his will. Our religion is more than theory. It is practical. The church must learn to express in conduct throughout the week the word heard on Sunday. There are numberless opportunities for service in the name of Christ. And while this type of evangelism is not subject to tabulation, I am convinced more and more that the church grows in the love and affections of people by the service rendered in the name of Christ even as much as it does by the message proclaimed on the Lord's Day.

6. *Vocational evangelism.*—I have never liked the term professional evangelism and I do not blame our brethren who give themselves to this work for resenting being called professional evangelists. This happy term, vocational evangelism, is coming into vogue and I would like to use it with such emphasis that others would join me in its use.

In the early church there were apostles, prophets, elders, deacons, and there were also evangelists. The New Testament seems to present this person as one who sets things in order. There is great need at the present stage of Christian development for this type of work. I hope many of our young men in colleges and universities today will dedicate themselves to the task of vocational evangelism.

We have engaged in recent years in a good deal of criticism of our evangelists and probably much of it has been justified. We have said that there has been too much anxiety to manipulate the adding machine and burn the wires with big reports. But when we have said the worst it is still a fact that we are today numerically at least what we are largely on account of the work of our evangelists. Let us be fair with these men who have been the recruiting servants of Jesus Christ; and if some of their methods have not been of the highest order, let us remember the kind of people with whom they have had to deal. They have had to handle us and this fact may account for a good deal of their procedure.

A friend of mine recently gave me what he regarded as a severe rebuke on the ground, that I was rapidly passing from the intellectual to the emotional and that I was losing some of my original dignity by advocating evangelism with such enthusiasm. Now, of course, I was complimented by the suggestion that I had ever been intellectual and appreciated the fact that at one time I did maintain a dignified mien; but I felt then and still feel that the church must enlarge her borders by evangelistic activity, and if we cannot get philosophers to do the work, we will have to take others.

The church will not be able to discard the special or vocational evangelist as long as our humanity is living in the abnormal state of sin. We may have an educational program carefully worked out and may have in active operation all of the elements thus far mentioned. But this will not reach a certain type of our adult citizenship and the church is not doing her duty if this field is left neglected. No program of evangelism through the ordinary channels of the church will meet the requirements of the day. In addition to this there ought to be the annual evangelistic campaign and community-stirring under the leadership of one who is filled with the spirit of Christ and who has the courage to challenge the crass, formal and materialistic tendencies of our modern life.

In a word I believe the evangelistic program

for today ought to include at least these six elements: the personal, educational, seasonal, architectural, social and vocational. Let each man in some way do the work of an evangelist.

RURAL REDEMPTION

And Jehovah God planted a garden eastward, in Eden; and
there he put the man whom he had formed.—Genesis 2:8.

There are two ways of looking at the problem
of rural redemption and I am very much
tempted to take the first.

During the past few years I have read at
least three dozen books on rural problems,
church and others; and naturally have a
complete theory of the whole affair. Just recently I had the privilege of going through
another that purports to have been written from
a strictly scientific viewpoint. This is one
phase and it is the easiest to discuss. There
isn't anything more to my taste than to seclude
myself from the world and write out a scientific
solution to a problem such as rural redemption.
The rule is, Make it hazy and helpful.

The other viewpoint is practical. It consists
in studying the problem one faces immediately.
This does not lend itself to poetic fancy nor
scientific accuracy. The philosopher and theo-
logian do not find it very satisfactory. But to
the man who deals with rural problems day by
day it comes to be the only one he can in conscience follow.

I repeat, therefore, that it would be a great

deal easier for me to give a speculative disquisition on rural redemption and the agencies of the same; but I have chosen to discuss the matter from a strictly practical point of view.

Agriculture was the first business of humanity. Horticulture was the first profession. God introduces himself, after establishing the fact of his creatorship, as being interested in both agriculture and horticulture. He planted a garden eastward in Eden. It was filled with flowers and fruits. He created man and gave him a task. He was to dress and keep the garden. In this way he was to have dominion.

Those who deal with rural problems have the undergirding of this notion, that they are handling the most primitive and fundamental of all the pursuits and professions of man.

In the making of civilization two forces are found: the soil and the soul. There has never been a great civilization anywhere on the earth that did not send its roots into a fertile soil. The early civilizations of the race were along streams or around bodies of water. We find such in the valleys of the Ganges, Euphrates, Nile and Jordan rivers. The Roman Empire was a rather wide fringe around the Mediterranean Sea. He who ignores the fact that the soil must furnish the sustenance of humanity misses one of the big issues of an evolving civilization.

But there has never been a great civilization that did not draw its inspiration from religion. Religion has been the mainspring of every action worth recording. It has written our poetry and sung our songs; it has delivered our orations and constructed our temples; it has produced our literature and written our laws; it has created our music and painted our pictures. Religion has been the inspiration of life in every realm.

In the development of the race two edifices stand side by side, the granary and the sanctuary. Men have filled their granaries with food and their sanctuaries have inspired them with idealism for the ways of progress. Whatever theory one may have, or whatever practical application he may make of that theory, he must always keep in mind the fact that in a growing civilization the granary and the sanctuary must stand side by side.

One of the best books on rural problems is that written several years ago by Warren H. Wilson entitled *Evolution of a Country Community*. The value of this book is that it presents the matter, not as a finished product, but as a growing concern. He traces the development of social life and community evolution and leads us to believe that better days are before us. One is always tempted to take Mr. Wilson's outline and dress it up in a new garb and claim it for his own; but the material of the book has probably become such common property among our leaders that this would be hazardous, so I merely call attention to its value and especially its viewpoint.

Somehow I am always afraid of those books that settle a thing just as I am suspicious of a community or an organization that has all its problems solved. Recently, I visited a little inland town in Central Illinois. The guide to tourists and investigators showed me the town and among other things called my attention to a big rock that has quite a notable history. Standing by this rock he said, "This town has two things on Chicago: First, it is older than Chicago; second, it is finished." I think it is. And the trouble is there are a good many communities that are likewise finished. The word I speak may be of little service to such; but I have a desire to help all, not hopeless.

One of the problems troubling us in Illinois, and I think it is pretty generally the case throughout the country, is that we have a form of landlordism harmful both to the country and town alike. When a farmer gets a small piece of land paid for, after a long period of hard

work, one of the greatest temptations is for him
to rent it out and go to town. However radical
this man may have been in politics or religion
he immediately becomes an enforced reactionary. The very force of circumstances makes
him such. He has to keep up the place in the
country and a home in town; a school in the
country and one in town; a church in the country (he says so at least) and one in town; roads
in the country and streets in town; a barn in
the country and a garage in town; he has to
paint buildings in the country and buildings in
town.

The very necessity of the case makes him a
conservative and he will oppose most any movement either in town or in the country that tends
to increase his taxes. Even if he keeps his membership in the country church, a thing that he
should not do at all except in very rare instances, he will give such a small contribution
to the country church, according to his means,
that in its result it will do more to discourage
tenant givers than it will do good as a contribution. In many instances it would be better for
the absent landlord to give nothing. If he gives
$10.00 a year to the country church, his tenant
will think he has done well if he gives the same.
If the landlord didn't give a cent the tenant
would give more than both of them do and feel

that he wasn't liberal either. This is one of our big problems that must be met in some way.

There is no particular occasion for moving to town. The retired farmer, with the advantages we have these days, can be more comfortable out on the home place than in any town I know of in Illinois. If he would spend the money fixing up his farm and making a home for himself in the country that he spends in town he would reduce his living expenses, add to the beauty of the country and make his farm worth a great deal more as a civilizing factor. With the telephone, radio, rural free delivery, sanitary provisions, concrete walks around the place and hard roads increasing so rapidly, a man really has all the advantages of the town several miles away from the court house square and he isn't bothered with a lot of things that annoy people in a little town. If we could put on a successful drive, not under the motto, "Back to the farm," because when a man has once moved away it is hard to get him back; but even under a more suggestive one, "Stay on the farm," we would help solve, not only the rural church problem, but many others along with it.

One of the most difficult things to contend with in the average town community is the influence of the retired farmer. It isn't because he is a mean or stingy man; but it is because the economic program he has decided to follow makes him a conservative on nearly every issue that comes up both in town and in the country. One of the most fundamental things in rural redemption is to get the redeemers themselves to stay at home and work at the job.

Another problem we meet in dealing with rural redemption is the school. We have grown eloquent in the past about the little red school-house and have talked as if it were the final form of educational procedure. Having been a country school-teacher and having noted the good work of this institution I would be unkind to criticize the past; but the little country school has served its day and it must cease to be. Every state in the union must find a way to consolidate its schools and give the children of the country the same advantages claimed for them in towns and cities. We are working at it in Illinois. Other states are further along than we are but many have not come up to our point. Let me call attention to the fact again, that in any solution we may have, some sort of plan for consolidated schools with a big efficient program must be included.

Again it is the problem of diversified farming. I hesitate to mention this because it is the refuge of other politicians every time unjust or degrading laws are passed against the farmer, but there is something in it after all. There are some counties in which wheat is the only crop that can be made to pay. In others, corn or cotton. But to go into a county whose soil is clay, and not a very good quality of that, and undertake to raise corn or wheat is to sin against the soil.

I have two counties in mind that illustrate my point. They are in a portion of Illinois, not famous for its fertility of soil, but both counties are reasonably prosperous. One county is the twelfth in the United States in the raising of poultry and has an ambition to be first. Preachers abound also. Slowly the county is adding to its dairy interest and in a short time the poultry and dairying business of that county will bring in as much money per acre as the richest agricultural county in the State of Illinois. In the other county when a drouth took nearly everything one of the leading citizens told me their hens kept them happy. Would it not be folly to destroy the prosperity of the egg business in an effort to raise nubbins? Diversified farming is one of the issues, not of politicians, but of farmers and we will get considerable help in the matter of rural redemption when we face the issue.

But I am to speak especially of the country church and its relationship to rural redemption. I have been asked frequently if the country church is dying. There are two answers to that question, Yes and No. In places it is dying and in other places it is the most hopeful institution we have.

I could give you a list of twenty-five country churches in Illinois, for instance, and after studying them it would be the unanimous opinion, that so far as this evidence is concerned, the country church is not only dying, but is actually dead, for we are losing some of our country churches. On the other hand, I could give you a list of twenty-five and tell you the story of their achievements and prospects and it would be easy to get a verdict that the country church is the liveliest issue before us. Now the country church is both dying and growing.

The truth of the matter is we have too many country churches. They were built at a time when denominational prejudice was at high-tide and when people walked to meeting or rode in wagons. Our country churches and our country schools are both products of another age. With our increased facilities for travel there is no necessity for so many country churches and many of them will disappear, it matters not how much care we devote to them.

If the affair is managed properly, however, they may disappear into other churches and in dying render a larger service than in living. Every State Missionary Society ought to have a department of abandoned churches and it ought to watch these declining institutions with great care. When the day is done and the work is over, a country church ought to have a peaceful hour in which to depart this life and in passing ought to leave the legacy of remaining strength to another church. This can be done and I take it that it can be done better by a State Missionary Society than by any other agency of the brotherhood. Understand, I do not advocate the closing up of a church until its work is done; but when it is, the disgrace that comes from a decaying church building, should be avoided by a decent and respectable funeral service.

I believe I have spoken of general interests sufficiently and have presented the negative side of the proposition to such an extent that you are ready for me to launch out upon the positive side of what we can do through the country and village church toward rural redemption. To this task I gladly devote my attention now and shall do my very best to speak a worth-while word to all interested in the subject.

1. *To redeem rural life we must make efficient a sufficient number of rural churches to do the work of the Kingdom.*

I have already stated that we have too many rural churches. There are portions of the country in which this is not true but throughout that section of America in which we have our major strength it is the case. In many counties where we have from fifteen to twenty churches our cause would be stronger and the churches would be more efficient and capable with the number reduced to ten or a dozen. To do this will require wise leadership and great caution. It will probably be done but it will be accomplished by the law of growth rather than by the application of mechanics.

Every successful church is an experiment station in rural redemption. A short time ago I was making an investigation of the conditions in one of the counties in Illinois where agriculture is not quite up to standard. There are many reasons for it but the chief one is the lack of a fertile soil. Along about two o'clock in the afternoon we passed a small farm that was very different in every respect from the balance of the farms we had inspected. I asked the driver to stop and said to him, "That is the best farm we have seen today." His response was very significant. He said, "That is an ex-

periment station of the University of Illinois."
I asked him what effect it had had upon the
community. He said the farmers who paid no
attention to lecturers and who make fun of literary farming would travel miles to study what
is done by this experiment station. It seems to
me that every country church is just this—an
experiment station in rural redemption.

The rural church of tomorrow will be more
concerned about Christ and character than
creeds and corner stones. This is no revolution-
ary statement I am making but a casual reading
of the signs of the times. We will not make
churches tomorrow. They will grow. They
will not be mechanical, but vital. We will pay
more attention to the biological principle than
to the ecclesiastical. Denominationalism is
without defense, especially when it is sectarian.
Whatever name it bears the rural church will
have to exalt Christ rather than its creed and
service rather than its corner stone.

2. *We must have buildings for our rural
churches that will serve as community centers.*

There are three types of church buildings and
they represent three ideas of religion. The community that believes in the ceremonial will erect
a cathedral-like structure. Those who have
only the creedal conception will be satisfied
with the rectangular building. But if the edu-

cational ideal becomes prominent the church will erect an educational plant. In rural communities it is especially important that we have educational plants. The building dedicated to religion must be, not only a place of worship, but a community center and an educational plant.

This is one of our biggest problems because of the difficulty we have in getting the average rural community to spend a sufficient amount of money to put the cause on a permanent basis. With very few exceptions the rural community that takes a sufficient interest in religion to put up a plant that meets the demands of the occasion has a prosperous church. In nearly all communities where the people are satisfied with the old methods and with religion propagated entirely by the lecture system the church is either going backward or is barely holding its own. More than the average man is willing to admit, religion depends upon the type of building that we dedicate to its service.

Here is an outline of a successful church that I make bold to give to all who are interested in the development of our rural churches. There is very little possibility of success without an educational program, a financial policy and a social outlook. This kind of a program is useful in the city but it is absolutely necessary in the country.

3. *We must recognize the fact in rural redemption that religion is social as well as individual.*

Protestantism is individualistic. It was born of this spirit. It has been prosecuted in the same way. To the making of creeds there is no end. Every effort to socialize religion is met with the argument that it cannot be done. I am perfectly aware of the fact that the thing cannot be completely accomplished in a single generation. Let us remember that we have been following an individualistic program for more than four hundred years, and that it is not going to be easy to get the rural church to realize that it has a message to the community as such as well as to the individual units of the same.

Such a church must keep in touch with all the forces and agencies of the country life movement. It was recently stated in a public meeting in our state by an aggressive religionist that the State University is one of the greatest factors in the interest of rural redemption. No one would undertake to claim that the State University is distinctively a religious institution, but its relationship to the life of the people makes it worth while for every preacher and other worker interested in religion to get in touch with the State University. In Illinois under the leadership of Dr. R. E. Hieronymus, Community Advisor of the University of Illinois, we have an agency that is doing a wonderful service for all who are interested in the country life movement and especially the church.

4. *The business side of religion must be developed.*

What I am about to say will apply to all churches, whether in the city or country; but it is especially important to give it consideration as we deal with the rural churches. There are three elements in the business program of the church: (1) The budget system; (2) The Every Member Canvass; (3) The duplex envelope.

It isn't easy to get a community to consider the budget plan when the philosopohy has been for a generation or two "all paid in, all paid out." But farmers and all who labor with them are beginning to understand the value of the budget for the home and business. And it will be a distinct advantage to our rural churches when they make a careful budget for the church. The Every Member Canvass can be made an accomplished fact in the country. It may not be as easy to do it as it is in the city and the method may have to be much different, but there are country churches that actually make a personal canvass of every member of the church. Above all things do not permit the father to make a pledge for the family. This will defeat the Every Member Canvass and it is one of the most harmful methods that our churches have had. The duplex envelope with its constant appeal to support the cause at home and abroad will create as much missionary spirit as well as personal loyalty to the local church as a half dozen sermons through the year. I insist, therefore, that one of the ways to make effective our rural churches is to budget the expenses, make the Every Member Canvass and introduce the duplex envelope system. This will make for business in the Kingdom, regularity in support and create a worshipful spirit.

5. *We must establish New Testament churches.*

It seems almost superfluous in a convention of this kind to give utterance to such a statement but I am wondering if it is not true that we need to make a new study of this whole matter of the New Testament church. It is possible for an institution to have the same organization that the New Testament church had and be as far from the ideals of the New Testament as night is from day. I hold to the accuracy of organization according to the New Testament pattern, but must maintain that without the spirit of the New Testament this organization is a mere machine.

New Testament Christianity is a life, a force. It is Christ expressed in the life of the age. But we are living in the twentieth century and New Testament Christianity must do the same thing for the twentieth century that it did for the first. It revolutionized things then. It must do so today. It spiritualized then. It must do so today. Within three centuries the little democratic church, animated by the Spirit of the living God, overthrew the mightiest empire man had ever founded. If given an opportunity it will again turn the world upside down. It will do us good, however, to think of this not only in terms of a universal transformation; but what it will actually do in a single community.

Christianity stands for universal benefit. The great word of the gospel is "whosoever." Come, all; and go, everybody. This is the program of Christianity. This was the plan of the primitive church. This must be the plan of every church "after the pattern."

And there is no place in the life of the world where that thing is needed any more than in our rural communities. I submit, therefore, that it is our business to establish and maintain free aggressive churches of Christ.

6. *The rural church must have a brotherly attitude toward all Christians.*

Denominationalism is here and it will stay awhile. It seems to me that it is many times more intense in the country than it is in town. A county-seat church will have its own constituency and, therefore, is not handicapped by sectarian rivalry like the church in the country. A county-seat church will have its crowd but the country church will have a crowd. There will be many kinds of faith in some of these and it is a tremendous problem to get any sort of fellowship in the work of the Kingdom.

A Christian will help anywhere and a Christian church will let anyone help. Hospitality is what we need. If we cannot establish free New Testament churches then "our plea" is a failure and we are in the way. Let us spend more time on the Way and less time in trying to find a way.

This message comes to a close with the abiding conviction that we have never tried our plea to the full extent of our ability. I am thinking of a number of communities in which we have the only church. Instead of modifying the conditions of membership in the church, as they are clearly revealed in the New Testament, suppose we put on a program big enough to challenge the interest and attention of the entire community. If we do we will make our work so effective and vital that those who are unwilling to enroll as members with us will be glad to work with us and through us to the accomplishment of the work of Christ.

A city church or one in a county seat may be sectarian and "get by"; but the only hope of a rural church is to have a program as large as the New Testament and as vital as the life of Christ. This is our plea to and for the rural church. We as a people may not be able to solve the problem of rural redemption, but with our plea for an open free New Testament church and with a desire and program for the restoration of apostolic Christianity, we will be able at least to render a helpful service.

I have no patent process for the redemption of our rural communities but believe the gospel there, if given a chance, will be the power of God unto salvation.

AN ANCIENT PROGRAM FOR THE
MODERN CHURCH

And ye shall be witnesses unto me both in Jerusalem, and in all Judea, and in Samaria, and unto the uttermost part of the earth.—Acts 1:8.

This has been one of the famous missionary texts throughout the Christian centuries. The beginning place is Jerusalem. The gospel goes throughout the homeland, into and across the neighboring land, and then to the uttermost part of the earth. But this is not exactly a missionary address in the sense in which we usually use that term.

What I want to do today is to call attention to some ways in which the church of Christ may bear testimony in the community as an institution. The business of the church is to bear witness to Christ. We have strong convictions as to how individuals may do this. We are not always clear on corporate testimony, that is, the testimony of the organization itself. The church then must bear witness.

The modern church needs three things, and in these it will bear valuable testimony to the power of the gospel and the mission of the church. The church needs an educational program; a financial policy; and the social outlook.

AN EDUCATIONAL PROGRAM

The Disciples of Christ are now a little more than one hundred years old. It has been one hundred and seventeen years since Thomas Campbell prepared and delivered his famous "Declaration and Address." We are just beginning to realize the full import of the tremendous awakening, in which what we call the Restoration Movement was born and a big impetus was given to the American Church.

Alexander Campbell was an educator. He was not in the strict sense of the term a popular preacher, but he was a great teacher. He started a religious newspaper and founded a Christian college. Alexander Campbell ventured out on the sea of journalism in the *Christian Baptist*. This paper was later discontinued in order that another, called *The Millennial Harbinger,* with a somewhat different spirit, might be launched. Alexander Campbell started a religious newspaper because he believed in the power of the printed page in the propagation of Christianity. He founded a Christian college, Bethany, from an educational standpoint, the mother of us all. This college was co-educational. He introduced the Bible as a textbook. Alexander Campbell started a college on such a basis and with such principles because he believed in the power of a trained leadership, both in the pulpit and in the pew, in the propagation of the principles of the gospel of Christ.

The Disciples from the very beginning have steadfastly proclaimed two things: (1) No man can become a Christian until he learns how; (2) No man can become a better Christian except as he learns the way of the Lord more perfectly. These two principles have been basic in all the work the Disciples have done. The early disciples were called Christians, first at Antioch. The word "disciple" means a leader. The particular meaning of this text is that the leaders were named the anointed ones. The church is called by many titles, but it is first and last a school. Jesus taught his disciples, and the business of the church is to teach.

This is the divine order—knowledge, truth, freedom. The first purpose of the church is to teach the truth of Christ. The church is an educational unity in religion, and the whole program must be organized around the idea of teaching. Here is a good text for us as we face this outstanding responsibility: And ye shall know the truth, and the truth shall make you free.—John 8:32.

A Financial Policy

The church needs a financial policy. A generation ago we declared, "Salvation is free."

The brethren believed the preachers. Even Alexander Campbell preached against a paid ministry. He called those who received compensation for their work "hirelings." We got started wrong. We did not put the emphasis upon compensating those who dedicated themselves to Kingdom extension. We were either not clear on stewardship, or deliberately ignored it. As a result in the early days of our work there was needless suffering on the part of those who preached the gospel because the brethren were not trained in the scriptural principle that the laborer is worthy of his hire.

Later on we began to get a vision and then we passed the hat. At the close of a revival meeting, or a Sunday visitation, the leading elder would say, "Brother So and So has come among us to serve. He has a large family. We must not send him home empty-handed, we will pass the hat." In some cases one was fortunate if he got his hat back. We did not get very far with the hat-passing proposition.

And then came another stage in which somebody said it was the business of the deacons to raise the funds for the church, and in an unguarded moment somebody else either invented or suggested the subscription list. The leading families would be parceled out among the deacons. The first half of the year was used in taking the pledges; the second half was used in collecting them. Nine-tenths of all the board meetings devoted the major part of their time to the very important question of how to meet the deficit.

At last we began to take ourselves seriously on the financial phase of the work. Then we discovered the tithe and great attention was given to it. All Bible students are familiar with the clear-cut distinctions between Moses and Christ; the law and the gospel; the old covenant and the new covenant. There is no doubt but that the Jews were required by their law to give much more than a tenth. The tithe means a tenth. They gave that much, but they gave more. In some cases it must have reached as high as one-third.

Now the question arose, and it is still up: Is the Christian required by legal enactment to give a tithe? Many will answer emphatically "No." We are not trying to defend the tithe as an institution. Nothing is to be gained by this form of legalism, but there is one question that we ought to settle, and do it at once. *If a Jew with his limited blessings and opportunities was required to give a tenth of his income to the cause of religion, what should the Christian give?*

It is our deliberate conviction that the proper place to begin the study of stewardship is with the tithe. Just as one reaches clearer conceptions of the Christian religion by going through the Old Testament, so he can reach truer conceptions of Christian stewardship by studying the Jewish tithe.

There is a New Testament rule for giving that is different from the tithe. It seems to be the fruitage of the tithe. Here is the text: "Now concerning the collection for the saints, as I have given order to the churches of Galatia, even so do ye. Upon the first day of the week let every one of you lay by him in store, as God hath prospered him, that there be no gatherings when I come." There are five things that ought to be said about this rule of New Testament giving.

1. *The occasion.*—Why should we give? Paul answers this in a general way. He says, "Now concerning the collection for the saints, as I have given order to the churches of Galatia, even so do ye." The Corinthian Christians were to take a collection for the saints. In other words they were to support the cause of Christ financially. Now, I suppose it would be possible to take this simple scriptural principle, and carry it to such an extreme that it would be hurtful to the truth. But I am sure that it

covers the whole ground of the occasion of Christian giving.

2. *Systematic.*—There was a time to give. It was "Upon the first day of the week." This day was different from the Jewish Sabbath. That was a day of rest. The Lord's Day is a day of activity. The Sabbath was the memorial of creation; the Lord's Day is the memorial of re-creation. It is a memorial of the risen Lord. It is the birthday of the church. It is the day for communion with him in the Lord's Supper. It was the day of meeting for the disciples. Hence from Paul's viewpoint Christians should bring their offering "Upon the first day of the week."

3. *Individual.*—Giving is not a family proposition. It is not a group service. The principle is, "Let every one of you lay by him in store." We must emphasize the pronoun "him." We need to underscore every one. Religion is individual. The church is a democracy. The day of patriarchal religion is over. National religion has come to an end. We give as individuals. It is just as much a part of the worship to give as it is to pray. The preacher cannot pray for his congregation, nor can the father give for his family. It is an individual matter.

4. *Proportionate.*—Here is where we have our difficulties. Paul admonishes us to give

"as God hath prospered him." This raises the question as to the two rules of giving in the Bible. The Old Testament rule is the tithe; the New Testament rule is according to your prosperity. The individual Christian in the final analysis must be the judge. He has to decide in the light of the world's needs; the Master's call; his own conscience; and what he has. But it is evident that the tithe is the minimum. May I repeat the question previously asked, "If the Jew with his limited blessings and opportunities was required to give a tenth of his income to the cause of religion what should the Christian give?" Make the tithe the minimum, but go beyond Judaism. Be a Christian in giving and give proportionately.

5. *The results.*—The result of this rule will be, "that there be no gatherings when I come." The average church does not like to be bothered with special collections. There is only one way to escape the special appeal and that is to have sufficient funds on hands to meet the needs of the hour and the legitimate calls that come. A church that has made a budget of its needs and reasonable responsibilities; made the Every Member Canvass thoroughly and complete; and then adopts the duplex envelope will be able to meet the reasonable demands upon a church;

and in the language of Paul "there will be no gatherings" when the call comes.

I would like, therefore, to close this suggestion as to a financial policy by repeating again what is to me one of the most remarkable texts in the New Testament, "Now concerning the collection for the saints, as I have given order to the churches of Galatia, even so do ye. Upon the first day of the week let every one of you lay by him in store, as God hath prospered him that there be no gatherings when I come."

A SOCIAL OUTLOOK

Christianity is a universal religion. This is a truth so plain that no proof need be submitted. The golden text of the Bible says, that "God so loved the world that he gave." He loved the whole world and he still loves it. His call is universal.

The only political unit the New Testament takes into account is the world. Some of us may limit our vision to a township, or a county; but the Bible teaches that Christ died to save the world. Emerson said, "New England has a township mind." One of two things must be true, either New England is a good deal larger than Mr. Emerson thought it was, or it has evangelized a large part of the country, for many of us have a township mind.

The New Testament is a universal book. In Matthew Christ is presented as the Messiah; in Mark as a Mighty King; in Luke as a Perfect Man; in John he is a Universal and Eternal Savior. The picture in the gospels is that of an ageless and eternal man.

The Book of Acts records the triumphs of religion that began in Jerusalem, went throughout Judea, into and beyond Samaria, and unto the uttermost part of the earth. Slowly a religion that embraced the world in its vision came to the consciousness of men.

Nearly all the books of the New Testament deal with this universal religion. Some from one viewpoint, some another. The great battle the early church had to make was to keep itself from being a sect of Judaism. This discussion is seen in Galatians, Ephesians, Romans and Hebrews. In Galatians we have liberty in Christ and it is universal liberty that is declared. In Ephesians the middle wall of partition between the Jew and Gentile is broken down in order that God might make of the two one new humanity and bring peace to the world. In Romans this universal thought is given in terms of the highest law. Hebrews presents it in the priestly function.

The ideal of the New Testament is an international fellowship without regard to race, color, caste or kind. Paul carried it even farther than this and says there is neither male nor female.

By social vision we mean the church must prosecute her work without the artificial distinctions of money, culture, education, class, or any other standard.

There are no masters and slaves; employers and employees; rich and poor; educated and uneducated so far as God's grace is concerned. The opportunites of the gospel belong to all. "For God so loved the world, that he gave his only begotten Son, that whosoever believeth in him should not perish, but have everlasting life."—John 3:16.

THE CHURCH FACING MODERN LIFE

Jesus Christ is the same yesterday and today, yea and for ever.—Hebrews 13:8.

There are churches and the Church. This is no place to discuss the theological meaning of these terms; but we are on safe ground when we say that everyone, regardless of his theological views or ecclesiastical connections, believes that the church of the New Testament is different from the various institutions and organizations we call churches. It would scarcely be safe to say that the church is the sum total of all churches; but it is perfectly correct and legitimate to say that the church of Christ includes all the essential and fundamental elements of all the Christian institutions of our age —and much more. In this address I would like to believe, therefore, that I have such a grasp of my problem that I can speak for all these. As we talk about the church facing modern life we mean the whole Church.

Life is an elusive term. Modern life is more so. One can live in this age and be an ancient. Modern life does not have to do entirely with time. He is a modernist who has profited by the achievements of the past; has a clear grasp of what is going on today; and believes in tomorrow. Most of us are modernists in varying degrees. Modern life is the sum total of the views, forces, institutions and agencies of our day. As the church faces this complex situation, her leaders are almost appalled by the multiplicity of things to consider and in some cases of contradictions, both apparent and real.

In spite of all this confusion there are clearly three things which we regard as the summary of modern life. We hope to discuss these and show the relationship of the church to them. To state the problem concretely modern life is sustained by three forces: (1) Democracy—the method of all social procedure. (2) Education —the plan for preparation. (3) A Christ-centered theology—the inspiration.

1. *Democracy is the method of present-day social procedure.*

There are two methods of human government, autocracy and democracy. Autocracy regulates from above. Democracy from below. Autocracy is efficient, capable and successful. Democracy wastes much time and energy in finding itself, and many times does not score what the world calls a success. But in spite of its weaknesses modern life accepts the theory of democracy and is more and more becoming democratic.

In recent years we have seen much of the triumph of democracy. Kings and queens, czars and kaisers have gone to the rubbish heap, or in the language of others, are now in the discard. We have reached the stage where we have but little more respect for a king than for a nine spot. All one has to do is to lift his eyes in any direction and he will observe the rising tide of democratic forces. This is true in China, Japan, India, Persia, Turkey, Russia, Germany and certainly in Britain and the United States. Both continents of the Western hemisphere, South America as well as North America, are in the very midst of a tremendous democratic awakening.

This principle is coming to manifest itself in commercial and industrial affairs as well as political. The great commercial enterprises of our day, in order to guarantee their future, are recognizing the principle of democratic procedure. One does not have to be a prophet to announce that this will become increasingly the case. Time will not permit a full discussion of the proposition announced, but it is so apparent that elaborate argumentation is unnecessary.

In religion the principle is specially manifest. Christianity in its organic forms presents a cross section, not only of humanity as it is throughout the earth today; but humanity longitudinally for two thousand years. In other words we have under the name Christian every form of government from the imperial autocracy of Rome to the disorganized mob in the small room on a side street of a great city. To the casual observer autocracy seems to have the sway, but he who would accept this as a conclusion would make a tremendous blunder. The Roman hierarchy under the influence of two forces, one within and the other without, is slowly yielding to the principle of modern democracy and ultimately it, too, will be democratic. All the religious bodies of the world and especially in America, are feeling the need of a larger degree of submission to this force.

The church is compelled to recognize this spirit, and will see sooner or later that its advantage as a community agency and as the inspiration of life, will be augmented by even an extreme view of the rights of democracy. To carry my principle to the logical conclusion, every community has a right under the instruction of Christian leaders, to form such organization or organizations, as will fit the community, and as will enable the church to properly function democratically in the inspiration and uplift of the people.

Many of our mistakes today are due to the

fact that outside organizations or external agencies dictate to local communities, and render spontaneous, voluntary, efficient religious life well-nigh impossible. If four little churches in a community undertake to get together on the basis of the simple New Testament message, they will not be able even to arrange for their preliminary conference without taking the matter up with overhead directors or ecclesiastical dignitaries. The Community Church Movement is not a success because of modern denominationalism. Nearly every union church enterprise has failed because of outside dictation. When the religious bodies of our day are ready and willing to let the people decide the matter, and from such voluntary associations as will enable them to function religiously, keeping in mind always the high and holy ideals of the New Testament, we may be able to have community churches and accomplish a number of other things very badly needed. In other words, the church in facing modern life, must recognize the growing force of democracy in different communities. It is easy to see that it is democratize or die. We will have many funerals of dead churches, but finally we will learn how to meet the issue. We will democratize.

2. *Education is the plan of modern life for preparation to meet its issues.*

I am using the term "education" in a broader sense than the technical and academic one. When the government would have a bond sale it must be introduced by a campaign of education. Commercial and industrial firms know the value of education and use this mighty force in great advertising campaigns. The item of advertising in the expense budget of a successful corporation is tremendous. A political campaign is an educational enterprise. Many times the things in which we are instructed have no value; but politicians recognize the fact that to get action from the people on any issue they must instruct, inspire and direct. In other words, educate.

In the things distinctly academic this principle is most marked. America has an educational program reaching from the kindergarten to the university. The plan of modern secular education is to take the citizen as soon as he becomes conscious of life, and by a process of training bring him out a finished product through kindergarten, grades, high school, university and even graduate courses. To attack the system of modern education is really to repudiate the achievements of a thousand years and undertake to turn back the tides of time.

It would be about as easy to change the stars in their courses or the sun in its orbit, as to reverse the educational processes of our day and adopt another principle of procedure.

Modern education does not date back two thousand years; but modern education did not begin with the date that marks modern history. I repeat the modern educational movement has been growing and unfolding for two thousand years or more. Our whole life is shot through and through with the conviction that the only way to get anything done at all is by a campaign of education.

The church must face this problem, and happy are we in the faith that the church is not only willing to face it, but actually created the situation itself.

Some time ago I heard a distinguished educator make the statement that modern education had created two concepts: (1) The unfolding child. (2) That one must teach out of his consciousness of the subject. I thought over these things for a while and then read the New Testament. I found that the two concepts, supposed to have been created by modern education, were really contributions of Jesus of Nazareth. In the manner of his development we find the model for an unfolding life. He increased physically, mentally, socially and spiritually. Luke tells us that he increased in wisdom and stature and in favor with God and man. His is the only normal development among the children of men. So natural and normal was his life that the only way we can understand him is to put him in a place by himself and call him the Supernatural Man. He was so natural that he becomes supernatural by contrast and comparison.

Then when he began his teaching he spoke out of the consciousness of God and the soul. It is said of him that he spoke as one *having* authority and not as the scribes. They were literalists and dogmatic. Their message was static and fixed. His was vital, dynamic, moral and spiritual. He spoke out of the fullness of his heart.

The church, therefore, has the two great principles upon which all education depends: (1) That a human soul is capable of natural, normal development and unfoldment. (2) That the teacher must teach out of the consciousness of the subject he presents.

Some of these days the church will accept her own program and when that day comes we will have a wonderfully enlarged outlook on life. When an educational program becomes the plan of the church, and it is very rapidly becoming so, ecclesiastical dictatorship, theological guessing and religious mechanics will be at an end; and the church will rely upon its conquest of the community and the world by a program of teaching.

Education is synthetic and unifying. The church never divides while it is learning. It is only when the church or a large majority of the membership has fixed and finished views on a subject that danger arises. The growing, developing minority finds it impossible to believe that the thing is finished, and by agitation disturbs the peace and harmony of the organization. The only cure for modernism is more modernism. The only cure for democracy is more democracy. The only cure for the difficulties that come from education is the adoption of a far-reaching and thorough plan that will make the church an educational unit in the religious life of the community.

The church must adopt a program of education. It is a significant fact that secular education has actually taken the plan of Christianity, and is now serving in the capacity of evangelist, offering the method of procedure to the creator of it. The church will finally win. In fact, is winning. In most communions religious education is the dominant note.

3. *A Christ-centered theology is the inspiration of modern life.*

To some of you it will be a rather hackneyed statement to say that Christianity is a Christ-centered religion. In its organic forms it has not always been such, and even now in many of its big denominational manifestations it is not. Very few of the discussions of Christendom have had to do with Christ. Some of them have appeared to be discussions about him, but upon close examination it will be found that our theological warriors have been fighting over an imaginary Christ.

The Bible has many messages, but one message, and that message is Christ. The word from the Mount of Transfiguration is the note of the hour, "Hear ye him." Jesus is neither an ancient, a medieval nor a modern. He is the timeless and ageless man. He is the God-man.

There are two ways of presenting religion. We can look at Christ through our doctrines and ceremonies. Many of us do this. This is neither the normal nor the Christian way. We must look at them through him. I am aware of the fact that the Bible tells the story of Christ but after the story has been told, we can understand it only as we look at it through him. We must study the ordinances and institutions of

Christianity through Christ. Then the church becomes the social expression of Christ. In fact, it actually and really becomes Christ himself.

THE DISCIPLES AND THESE PRINCIPLES

Are we as a people prepared by our principles and our historic setting to meet the issues of the hour and adopt these three great principles of modern life? A careful study of the life and labors of Alexander Campbell will prove that he had much to do with the present movement so manifest in these three particulars.

1. Alexander Campbell stood for the absolute democracy of the local congregation. In fact, he carried this to such an extreme that many of the churches formed under his teaching were not able to stem the tide because they lacked social solidarity. A study of the *Christian Baptist* and the *Millennial Harbinger* will reveal much by way of absolute democracy, pure and unadulterated. Those who labored with Alexander Campbell espoused this cause and if there is any one thing that is distinct among our people today it is the independency of the local congregation.

2. Alexander Campbell was a pioneer in the field of religious education. He founded a college and made the Bible a textbook in that in-

stitution. His chapel lectures were not pietistic
talks but great educational messages to college
men and women. He founded a religious newspaper and kept the printing press running constantly. He believed personally in two things:
(*a*) The value of trained leadership in the
Kingdom of God. (*b*) The power of the printed
page in the propagation of the principles of
that Kingdom. Every preacher that went out
in those early days proclaimd two things: (*a*)
No man can become a Christian until he learns
how. (*b*) No man can become a better Christian except as he learns the way of the Lord
more perfectly. Alexander Campbell called his
brethren disciples of Christ and looked upon
them as learners in the school of Jesus. The
movement he launched was a pioneer in the field
of religious education.

3. Alexander Campbell certainly preached a
Christ-centered theology. Martin Luther stood
for the open Bible; John Calvin for the sover-
eignty of God; John Wesley for the work and
operation of the Holy Spirit; and Alexander
Campbell for the centrality of Jesus in the
Christian message. Early in his preaching this
was manifest. A climax was reached in 1816
when he delivered his memorable sermon on the
law showing the difference between the old and
new and calling attention to the place of Christ

in the plan of the ages. His was clearly a Christ-centered theology and it has ever been the program of the Disciples of Christ to exalt him above all others.

It is not my contention that we have been perfect in maintaining these principles, but without a doubt we have made a distinct contribution to the democracy of religion, to religious education and to a Christ-centered theology. It seems to me that our people have a great mission to perform in this age when men are talking community interests and are inclined to the simple forces we have been trying to present and which are expressed in our religious body to a remarkable degree. It is altogether possible to establish open, free New Testament churches and to leave them unhampered and uncontrolled by alien and outside agencies. For such a task we were born.

Conclusion

The problems and principles I have been discussing today have to do with the open country, the village and the city. Conditions vary, but life is the same. We are especially concerned, however, with rural communities. I do not undertake to settle questions for those of you who are especially concerned, however, with rural communities. I do not undertake to settle questions for those of you who are specialists and experts in rural life; but I give you in this closing word the convictions of my life, that democracy, education and a Christ-centered theology are the hope of the rural community and the modern world.

A PERSONAL WORD

The address which follows is clearly "shop talk" and no attempt has been made to cover up this fact. The writer has been the State Secretary of the Illinois Christian Missionary Society for eleven years. He has spent one-third, and the best one-third, of his ministry in this service and believes in it as never before.

Those who have read the chapters leading up to this will be prepared to read "The Place of the State Missionary Society," which is an effort on the part of a State Secretary through the organization that supports him, and through which he and many others operate, to bring into actual realization the things advocated. From this standpoint we are confident the readers will find a high degree of delight in this chapter.

H. H. PETERS.

THE PLACE OF THE STATE MISSIONARY SOCIETY

The text for this address is from the Book of Common Experience, "Charity begins at home." The revised version of said text adds, "But does not end there."

Dr. E. I. Osgood in the opening paragraph of his book, *China's Crossroads,* has an interesting statement with which I can easily begin this message: "A man thinks in a language. The language in which he thinks is usually the same one in which he makes known his thoughts to others. His thinking is colored by the books he reads, the community in which he lives and by the familiar objects which he daily sees. He thinks in terms of the community, the state or nation in which he lives or works. If he makes a tour of the globe, everything he sees is colored by the sights with which his eyes have been familiar since childhood. He is comparing every new thing with similar conditions in his home community or state. He is merely reasoning from the known to the unknown."

This describes my situation almost exactly. I have a State Missions complex. I have been State Secretary in Illinois for ten years and naturally my sight is colored by two things:

(1) The office of State Secretary. (2) The office of State Secretary in Illinois. But in this message on "The Place of the State Missionary Society," I shall do my best to dissolve this complex and speak in terms as universal as possible.

Does the State Missionary Society have a place in the organized life of our brotherhood? I would like to emphasize the word "organized" in this question. Of course it is utterly impossible to limit our organized activities to two agencies; but so far as the major work of the Disciples is concerned, it is confined to the United Christian Missionary Society and the Board of Education of the Disciples of Christ. We have some minor organizations and a large number of independent agencies appealing to us for help, and in addition to all this we have the International Convention of the Disciples of Christ.

In the midst of this is the State Society, or it would be better to say, a large number of state and provincial societies. Now the question again: Does a State Society have any place in this organized life?

Do we need an organization to function in a definite capacity within the state? Or, is it possible for the above-mentioned national and international organizations and agencies to handle the problems that are of state significance? I have already admitted that I have a State Missionary complex; and therefore my answer is anticipated. But I will have to show a reason for the hope that is within me in order to establish the claim that is about to be made.

I believe we need State Societies, and I would define such a society as a state-wide efficiency organization for constructive and reconstructive evangelism. Now, I am not arguing for uniformity among the state organizations. We have twenty-five states that ought to have independent State Missionary Societies, probably more; and then we have large sections of the country that can be combined under provincial or regional organizations. My definition of the State Society would include the latter as well as the former. A State Society does not necessarily have to be entirely autonomous to come within the purview of my definition; but it is my judgment that wherever it is possible the State Society should be entirely independent, free from all other agencies and activities, and I believe I would go far enough to say that provincial and regional groups could be independent of other organizations to the advantage of the cause.

There are two forms of government, autocracy and democracy. Autocracy governs from above; democracy governs from below. One goes from the top down; and the other goes from the bottom up. In religion we find these two principles of government in very pronounced forms. We have every shade of governmental manifestation from one extreme to the other. In other words, in organized religion, we have all forms of government from the highly centralized autocracy of the Roman Catholic Church to the independent group of Disciples that refuses to recognize any principle of authority, co-operation or fellowship.

Our brotherhood theoretically is neither autocratic nor anarchistic. It is not a monarchy, nor is it a group of independent soviets. Ours is a constructive, co-operative, voluntary democracy. We can only move and act as a people as we are willing to think together, talk together, work together and live together.

Our movement is from one viewpoint a great experiment in religious democracy. Other bodies of religionists deliberately maintain the monarchistic or aristocratic form of government; but we have declared to the world in no uncertain sound that we believe in the principle of democracy in religion and our present effort is an experiment in that field. If we can establish the authority of Christian co-operation and can maintain intact an organization that will function effectively without delegated authority, ours will be one of the most important achievements in the history of organized religion.

It is possible for us to have such a co-operative democracy as begins in the county, goes through the state, and throughout the nation into international relationships. In order to function effectively it must be free and independent, be open and above board in all its relationships and further the work of all co-operative efforts.

An institution of any kind is known by the problems it honestly faces and tries to solve. I would like to call attention to a number of these problems which are squarely up to such an institution as a State Missionary Society.

1. *Locating preachers.*—Everybody who has given this matter any thought at all knows that one of the biggest problems before our people today is that of bringing church and preacher together. There is no agency among us working definitely at that task except the State Missionary Society, and while many of our State Secretaries would be glad to "pass the buck," and turn the matter over to others, it is fundamentally our job until a better program can be worked out. I am quite well acquainted with one secretary that had more than three hun-

dred applications in five months and these months included the summer season. These applications came at a time when the churches wanted to wait until the fall work opened up and when all the preachers seemed to want to move before school opened. It surely was a merry time in that office, and many a day the overworked secretary would have been delighted, and he came very nearly doing it, to throw the whole batch of applications into the waste basket, lift his hands as high in the air as possible, and holler, "Enough"; but the work went on and the issue was honestly faced. No State Secretary can guarantee a position to any preacher. It would be utterly impossible for the strongest State Secretary, backed by the most thoroughly organized State Society in the brotherhood, to guarantee even a third-rate job to the Pope of Rome, the Archbishop of Canterbury, or the ablest orator among the Disciples of Christ. A State Society is merely a matrimonial agency, lending its office to introducing and cultivating courtship between church and preacher. It is a big job but an interesting one.

2. *Forming pastoral unities.*—I shall be compelled in this address to refer to things that have happened in my own experience in Illinois, and I am doing so with the feeling that the problem is just about the same in other states.

We have seven hundred churches in Illinois. Only three hundred of these are full-time churches. The other four hundred are part-time churches, ranging all the way from no preaching or occasional preaching to a few that have three-fourths time. After we have helped student preachers find employment, and men who are engaged in other work, to connect up with part-time churches, there remains a large number of churches in Illinois, and probably most other states, that cannot be provided for by such non-resident service as we know about. These churches could be grouped into unities. Sometimes four constitute a pastoral unity but usually two rather substantial part-time churches are sufficient. It is my sincere hope that every State Missionary Society may carry on a vigorous campaign for the formation of pastoral unities so that we may have a large number of our ablest men preaching for two or more churches in contiguous territory.

3. *Taking care of abandoned church property.* —In one state that I could mention in all probability more than two hundred churches have been abandoned and their property sold or disposed of in some way. Some of the money has gone into the enterprises of the Kingdom, but without a doubt a great deal of money from abandoned churches has gone into useless en-

terprises. Some of it may have gone into the purses of brethren to reimburse them for funds they imagined they were giving to the cause of Christ. The State Missionary Society is the proper organization to lead out in the matter of caring for abandoned churches. Some states have a highly developed plan and others are lagging behind. It would not be difficult to put on a carefully worked out program to take over all abandoned property and close it up decently and in order. In Illinois wherever we are permitted to do so we close up such properties and hold the money in the treasury of our Permanent Fund as a named fund; and we agree that if the church should ever be revived in that particular neighborhood and a building erected, we will turn the money back to apply on the building.

4. *Helping finance local churches.*—One of the most pitiable things we have to meet in our work today is the inability of some of our churches that are supposed to have plenty of resources to finance themselves. Until recently our strongest churches did not work out a careful budget. If the Every Member Canvass was made at all it was made in a rather slipshod way. Among our best organized churches we are rapidly coming to three things: 1. The budgeting of church obligations; 2. The Every

Member Canvass; 3. The duplex envelope. The State Society by its office and field force can help materially in bringing all of our churches to a higher degree of efficiency. I recently had the privilege of giving a young preacher some advice which gained me the reputation of being both a legalist and a literalist; but I have ceased to worry about titles of that kind, and so I am going to incorporate that advice in this address. I said to him, "Keep the baptistry wet and the money coming in." This is neither the time nor the place to go into details as to how the State Society can help get our churches on their feet financially, but it can be done.

5. *Raising church debts.*—One of the easiest things to do is to pay off a church debt if somebody comes along with a plan that has religious inspiration and business sagacity in it. The State Secretary is supposed to deal in both of these. Many of our churches drag along through the years under the burden of a debt, and it doesn't matter how big or how small it is the effect is the same. The State organization with its force should resolve itself into an agency for the elimination of all old church debts, and have an equally vigorous plan for getting the churches to make new ones for new churches, or extensive improvements, or a parsonage, or something else.

6. *Dedicating built or rebuilt churches.*—I have had quite a bit of experience during the past few years in conducting building campaigns, in raising church debts and in dedicating built or rebuilt churches. There is a good deal of "mystery" about these things that should be eliminated. It does not take a financial wizard, nor a promotional genius, to dedicate a church. I would be somewhat inclined to magnify this task out of all proportions in order that I might create the impression that the brotherhood is dependent upon a few of us to dedicate all the churches. There are some professional dedicators, and I am a hundred per cent for them, and after all of us have done our dead level best in our respective fields there will be enough left to keep any group of professional dedicators that we may have as busy as bees.

7. *Organizing city missionary societies.*—We crave efficiency. Sometimes we dislike the idea of dividing honors within our state. It is nevertheless a fact that many large city centers can be evangelized and developed better by city missionary societies, organized under the direction of, and in co-operation with the State Society, than otherwise. In Illinois we have six city missionary societies. We have been able in these centers to do much more work with

them and through them than we would have done otherwise. This problem will have to be worked out by each state according to its centers of urban population.

8. *Securing the services of pastors of large churches to be big brothers toward near-by needy fields.*—The pastor of a large church is always a busy man but he cannot afford to neglect the opportunities for gospel extension in the schoolhouses and vacant churches near his center of activity. There are always needy fields contiguous to a large church. Some of these are schoolhouses, where Sunday schools can be conducted. There are usually some vacant churches or churches inactive most of the time. These afford the opportunity for the pastor of the large church to do some fundamental missionary work. These small churches cannot raise much money and their members constantly move to town. They are therefore mission points but if neglected the effect will tell upon the town or city church nearest.

9. *Arranging for volunteer evangelistic meetings.*—We will never be able to raise enough money through the State Missionary Society, however efficient it may be, or capable as a collecting agency, to employ evangelists enough to cover the whole field. Ten pastors, each holding a volunteer meeting, are the equivalent of

an employed State Evangelist, and the work they do is worth more to the cause than any ten meetings a State Evangelist could hold. The State Secretary should encourage the holding of volunteer meetings.

10. *Reviving inactive churches.*—It would be foolish to revive some inactive churches. Others should be revived and that speedily. Some of each kind are in villages, towns and cities. The big problem of the inactive church, however, has to do with the country church. There are two types of these. There are country churches toward which the people naturally gravitate for their social functions. In all such places it is possible to maintain a live wire church. Then there are other communities in which the people seem to move away from the church for their social life and activity. In such cases it is very difficult to keep the church alive. In reviving country churches I would suggest that a careful study be made of community tendencies. It may be that the abandoned church, or the inactive one, has no longer a field.

11. *Advising preachers about literature.*—A circulating evangelistic library is a good thing. In fact, a circulating library of any kind for preachers and church workers has distinct value. Suggestions as to what to read, and

even the preparation of lists of books, have a place in the State Missionary program.

12. *Establishing new churches in strategic fields.*—The most advantageous fields today for the establishment of new churches are in large cities and towns where we have not entered and in suburban districts. The major part of our evangelistic activity so far as new churches are concerned can be expended in communities of this character. There are not many opportunities for the establishment of country churches in many of the states in which we are numerically strong. A large amount of work, however, can be done to a good advantage in developing some of the most important fields we have in the country.

13. *Maintaining fellowship with our educational agencies.*—The State Society that does not interest itself in the educational agencies of the brotherhood within its territory is making a mistake. What is the use to raise money to hold meetings and organize and develop churches without preachers to take charge of them or trained leaders to carry on the program? We have run across a few instances in recent years in which the feeling was quite general that every dollar appropriated to the college within the state was taken from the State Missionary budget. This is a shortsighted

view of the situation. The college and other educational agencies within the state are portions of the machinery of the State Missionary Society and the co-operation ought to be intimate and complete.

14. *Promoting conventions.*—Our people like to attend conventions and they enjoy hearing big sermons and great speeches. A series of county conventions is a wise procedure. These ought to be held in the summer season. The old-fashioned basket dinner and open air meeting should be important features of all these gatherings. A uniform county organization is questionable but some kind of co-operative fellowship is worth while. Most states can also hold a series of district conventions at strategic times and places to the good of the cause. These county and district conventions, together with the state convention, enable the leaders of the State Missionary Society to reach the entire constituency. The order is, county, district, state and nation.

15. *Maintaining fellowship with our national and international agencies.*—Attention has already been called to the fact that it is the business of the State Society to co-operate fully and freely with the regular national and international interests of the brotherhood. Charity may begin at home, but it does not end there.

This is a brotherhood and co-operation and not competition should be the rule.

This is a good place to repeat the definition of a State Missionary Society. It is a state-wide efficiency organization for constructive and reconstructive evangelism.

To accomplish these things, and such other items as may come up from time to time, the office and field force of the State Society ought to stand for the following definite principles:

1. Loyalty to the organized activities of the brotherhood, promotional, missionary and educational.

2. Faithfulness to all the churches, whether large or small, in the country or in cities. All churches should be included in the scope of the State Missionary program.

3. A brotherly attitude toward the entire ministry, refusing to recognize parties, groups or cliques. We are passing around such names as liberal and conservative; progressive and reactionary; radical and fixed; modernist and fundamentalist. This business of classification is largely nonsense.

4. A refusal to be a theological institution, or an ecclesiastical agency, and to recognize or create tests of orthodoxy and fellowship. Uni-

formity of thinking cannot be maintained. Somebody will break over just for the sake of the exercise he gets out of it, if for no other reason. The Missionary Society should stay at its task and let the brethren browse around.

5. And then after all has been said and done, every person in the employ of a State Society ought to be reasonably familiar with the history of the Disciples of Christ, the principles for which they stand, and help in every way in the symmetrical development of our people.

A State Missionary Society is a state-wide efficiency organization whose objective is constructive and reconstructive evangelism.